T0131264

Genetic
Engineering in
Agriculture

Genetic Engineering in Agriculture

The Myths,
Environmental Risks,
and Alternatives

SECOND EDITION

Miguel A. Altieri

FOOD FIRST BOOKS
OAKLAND, CALIFORNIA

Copyright © 2004 Institute for Food and Development Policy. All rights reserved. No part of this book may be reproduced or transmitted in any form or by any means, electronic or mechanical, including photocopying, recording, or by any information storage retrieval system, without written permission from the publisher, except for brief review.

Printed in Canada

Text design by Amy Evans McClure
Cover design by Stephen Hassett

Food First Books
398 60th Street
Oakland, California 94618
www.foodfirst.org

Library of Congress Cataloging-in-Publication Data on file with publisher

Food First Books are distributed by:
CDS at (800) 343-4499

10 9 8 7 6 5 4 3 2 1

Contents

Preface

Dr. Peter Rosset, former codirector of Food First, and I organized the International Workshop on the Ecological Impacts of Transgenic Crops, held at the Berkeley campus of the University of California on March 2–4, 2000. This workshop was cosponsored by Food First and the Center for Biological Control of UC Berkeley, with the generous support of the Foundation for Deep Ecology, the Fred Gellert Family Foundation, the Consultative Group on International Agricultural Research (CGIAR), and a private anonymous donor.

The workshop was attended by twenty-one scientists from universities (UC Berkeley, UC Santa Cruz, Cornell University, Guelph University, Iowa State University, Ohio State University, University of Minnesota, Swiss Federal Institute of Technology, Elmhurst College, and Open University in the UK), international agricultural research centers (Centro Internacional para Mejoramiento de Maíz y Trigo [CIMMYT/International Maize and Wheat Improvement Center] in Mexico, Centro Internacional de la Papa [CIP/International Potato Center] in Peru), nongovernmental organizations (Union of Concerned Scientists, Food First, Consumers Union, and Assistance and Services for Alternative Agriculture Projects/AS-PTA Brazil), and a private organization (Dynamac Corporation).

We thank the donors for their support for the event and this report, and also all those who attended and provided many insights into the complex issues surrounding the environmental impacts of agricultural biotechnology. The report from this workshop provided extensive material for this book.

Introduction

In the last decade, a debate began around the applications of biotechnology in agriculture. Many questions arose: Who benefits from the technology? What are the environmental and health impacts? To whose needs does biotechnology respond? How does the technology affect what is being produced, how it is being produced, and for what and for whom? What are the social, ethical, and ecological criteria that guide research choices in agricultural biotechnology? What alternatives have been foregone?

To many people the domination of agricultural research agendas by commercial interests, the uneven distribution of benefits, especially for poor farmers, the possible environmental risks, and the exploitation of the Third World's genetic resources demand a deeper inquiry. The poorest are actually the ones who lose, as biotechnology exacerbates trends toward industrialization of agriculture, erodes the diversity of agroecosystems, and undermines the rights of farmers. For me a key problem facing the public is that biotechnology companies and associated scientific bodies are making false promises that genetic engineering will move agriculture away from a dependence on chemical inputs, reduce environmental problems, and solve world hunger. Such promises are founded on philosophical and scientific premises that are fundamentally flawed, and these premises need to be exposed and criticized in order to advance toward a truly sustainable agriculture.

BACKGROUND

Until about four decades ago, crop yields in US agriculture depended on internal resources: recycling of organic matter, built-in biological control mechanisms, and rainfall patterns. Agricultural yields were modest but stable. Production was safeguarded by growing more than one crop or variety in space and time in a field, as insurance against pest outbreaks or severe weather. Nitrogen was replaced in the soil by rotating major field crops with legumes. Rotations suppressed insects, weeds, and diseases by effectively breaking the life cycles of these pests. A typical Corn Belt farmer grew corn in rotation with several crops, including soybeans, and small grain production was intrinsic to maintain livestock. Most of the labor was done by the family who owned the farm, with occasional hired help. No specialized equipment or services were purchased from off-farm sources (Altieri 1995).

In the developing world, small farmers developed even more complex and biodiverse farming systems, guided by indigenous knowledge that has stood the test of time (Thrupp 1998). In this type of farming, the link between agriculture and ecology was quite strong, and signs of environmental degradation were seldom evident.

But as agricultural modernization progressed, the ecology-farming linkage was often broken as ecological principles were ignored or overridden. Profit, rather than people's needs or environmental concerns, has shaped agricultural production. Agribusiness interests and prevailing policies favored large farm size, specialized production, crop monocultures, and mechanization.

Today monocultures have increased dramatically worldwide. Ninety-one percent of the 1.5 billion hectares of cropland is planted in monocultures to single crops such as wheat, rice, maize, cotton, and soybean at the expense of forests and wildlife habitat. Monoculture has implied the simplification and loss of biodiversity, the end result being an artificial ecosystem requiring constant human intervention in the form of agrochemical inputs, which, in addition to temporarily boosting yields, result in a number of undesirable environmental and social costs. Aware of such impacts, several agricultural scientists have arrived at a general consensus that modern agriculture confronts an ecological crisis (Conway and Pretty 1991).

The yearly loss of yields due to pests in many crops (reaching about 30 percent in most crops), despite the substantial increase in the use of pesticides (about 490,000 tons of active ingredient worldwide) is a symptom of the environmental crisis affecting agriculture. Cultivated plants grown in genetically homogenous monocultures do not possess the necessary ecological defense mechanisms to tolerate the impact of outbreaking pest populations (Altieri 1994).

When these agricultural models were exported to developing countries through the so-called Green Revolution, environmental and social problems were exacerbated. Most resource-poor farmers of Latin America, Asia, and Africa gained very little from the process of development and technology transfer of the Green Revolution, as proposed technologies were not scale-neutral. Farmers with larger and better-endowed lands gained the most, but farmers with fewer resources who were located in marginal environments often lost, and income disparities were often accentuated (Conway 1997). Guided by a Malthusian bias, the Green Revolution sought to fight food shortages by increasing food production through technological innovations. It failed because this approach ignored structural solutions to poverty and food scarcity. By favoring technological solutions the Green Revolution was not just involved with producing more food but also in creating a new global food system committed to the further industrialization of agriculture. Biotechnologists have yet to explain how genetically engineered crops can resolve the problems facing poor farmers, and they have also failed to address the complex and intractable issues of poverty and access to land.

Technological change has mainly favored the production of export or commercial crops produced primarily in the large farm sector, with a marginal impact on productivity of crops for food security, which are largely grown by the peasant sector (Pretty 1995). In areas where conversion from subsistence to a cash agricultural economy progressively occurred, a number of ecological and social problems became evident: loss of food self-sufficiency, genetic erosion, loss of biodiversity and traditional farming knowledge, and permanence of rural poverty (Conroy et al. 1996).

In order to sustain such agro-export systems, many developing countries have become net importers of chemical inputs and agricultural machinery, increasing government expenditures and exacerbating technological dependence. For example, between 1980 and 1984, Latin America imported about US $430 million worth of pesticides and used about 6.5 million tons of fertilizers (Nicholls and Altieri 1997). Such massive use of agrochemicals led to a major environmental crisis of yet unmeasured social and economic proportions.

THE FALSE PROMISES OF BIOTECHNOLOGY

What is ironic is that the same economic interests that promoted the first wave of chemical-based agriculture are now celebrating and promoting the emergence of biotechnology as the latest "magic bullet." Biotechnology, they say, will revolutionize agriculture with products based on nature's own methods, making farming more environmentally friendly and more profitable for farmers and healthy and nutritious to consumers (Hobbelink 1991).

The global fight for market share is leading major corporations to massively deploy genetically engineered (GE) plants (also known as genetically modified [GM] or transgenic crops) around the world (more than 145 million acres in 2002) without proper advance testing of short- or long-term impacts on human health and ecosystems. This expansion has been helped along by marketing and distribution agreements entered into by corporations and global food marketers (i.e., Ciba Seeds with Growmark, and Mycogen Plant Sciences with Cargill) and the absence of regulations in many developing countries.

In the US, the policies of the Food and Drug Administration (FDA) and Environmental Protection

Agency (EPA) consider genetically modified crops to be "substantially equivalent" to conventional crops. These policies have been developed in the context of a regulatory framework that is inadequate and, in some cases, completely absent.

The agrochemical corporations who increasingly control the direction and goals of agricultural innovation claim that genetic engineering will enhance the sustainability of agriculture by solving the very problems affecting conventional farming, and will spare the developing world from low productivity, poverty, and hunger. They claim that countries that embrace this superior agricultural technology will enjoy unprecedented prosperity, abundant and affordable food supplies, and reduced destruction of wild lands (Prakash and Conko 2004).

The objective of this book is to challenge the false promises made by the genetic engineering industry, by confronting myth with reality. The industry has promised that genetically engineered crops will move agriculture away from a dependence on chemical inputs, increase productivity, decrease input costs, and help reduce environmental problems (Office of Technology Assessment 1992). By challenging the myths of biotechnology, we expose genetic engineering for what it really is: another technological fix or "magic bullet" aimed at circumventing the environmental problems of agriculture (which are the outcome of an earlier round of technological fixes) without questioning the flawed assumptions that gave rise to the problems in the first place (Hindmarsh 1991). Biotechnology promotes single gene solutions for problems derived from ecologically unstable monoculture systems designed on industrial models of efficiency. Such a unilateral and reductionist approach has already proven ecologically unsound in the case of pesticides, whose promoters espoused a reductionist approach, using one chemical–one pest as opposed to the one gene–one pest approach now promoted by biotechnology.

The alliance of reductionist science and multinational monopolistic industry will take agriculture further down a misguided road. Biotechnology perceives agricultural problems as genetic deficiencies of organisms and treats nature as a commodity, while making farmers more dependent on an agribusiness sector that increasingly concentrates power over the food system.

CHAPTER ONE

Biotechnology, World Hunger, and the Welfare of Farmers

HUNGRY PEOPLE IN THE MIDST OF PLENTY

Biotechnology companies often claim that genetically modified organisms (GMOs)—specifically genetically altered seeds—are essential scientific breakthroughs needed to feed the world and reduce poverty in developing countries. Most international organizations charged with policies and research to enhance food security in the developing world echo this view. This view rests on two critical assumptions: that hunger is due to a gap between food production and human population density or growth rate and that genetic engineering is the best or only way to increase agricultural production to meet future food needs.

To clarify these misconceptions, it is important to understand that there is no relationship between the prevalence of hunger in a given country and its population. For every densely populated and hungry nation like Bangladesh or Haiti, there is a sparsely populated and hungry nation like Brazil or Indonesia. The world today produces more food per inhabitant than ever before. Enough food is available to provide 4.3 pounds for every person every day—2.5 pounds of grain, beans, and nuts; about a pound of meat, milk, and eggs; and another pound of fruits and vegetables (Lappé et al. 1998).

In 1999 enough grain was produced globally to feed a population of eight billion people (six billion inhabited the planet in 2000) had it been evenly distributed or not fed to animals. In the US alone, seven out of every ten pounds of grain are fed to animals. Countries such as Brazil, Paraguay, Thailand, and Indonesia devote thousands of acres of agricultural land to produce soybeans and manioc for export to feed cattle in Europe. By channeling one third of the world's production of grain from livestock to needy people, hunger would cease immediately (Lappé et al. 1998). Clearly, something is fundamentally wrong with the current food system. Despite greatly increased agricultural productivity, no less than 900 million people remain hungry and malnourished. Further, one in seven people in industrialized countries eat too much or make nonnutritious food choices that have led to a dramatic rise in obesity, heart disease, and diabetes.

Hunger is also compounded by globalization, especially when developing countries embrace the free trade policies advocated by international lending agencies, lowering tariffs and allowing goods from industrialized countries to flow in. The experience of Haiti, one of the world's poorest countries, is illuminating. In 1986 Haiti imported just 7,000 tons of rice, with the majority of rice consumed being grown on the island. After Haiti opened its economy to the world, cheaper rice immediately flooded in from the US, where the rice industry is subsidized. By 1996 Haiti imported 196,000 tons of foreign rice at the cost of US $100 million a year. Haitian rice production became negligible once the dependence on foreign rice was complete. The cost of rice rose, leaving large numbers of poor people at the whim of rising world grain prices. Hunger increased (Aristide 2000).

The real causes of hunger are poverty, inequality, and lack of access to food and land. Too many people are too poor (about two billion survive on less than one dollar a day) to buy the food that is available but often poorly distributed, or they lack the land and resources to grow it themselves (Lappé et al. 1998). In general, the food production–population ratio does not necessarily indicate that famine will occur. Famines have occurred in Asia during periods of high agricultural output and were due to speculative stockpiling, unemployment, and low purchasing power, not food shortages. When the true root cause of hunger is inequality, then any method of boosting food production that deepens inequality will fail to reduce hunger. Conversely, only technologies that have positive effects on the distribution of wealth, income, and assets, that are pro-poor, can truly reduce hunger. Fortunately, such technologies do exist, and can be loosely grouped together under the discipline of agroecology, the potential of which has been amply demonstrated (Altieri et al. 1998; Uphoff and Altieri 1999) and will be analyzed more fully later in this book.

Attacking inequality head-on by true land reform holds the promise of productivity gains far outweighing the potential of agricultural biotechnology which, so far, lacks the capacity to produce food where the poor and hungry live. Biotech proponents, however, argue that more than three quarters of the 5.5 million growers who benefit from bioengineered crops are resource-poor farmers cultivating about thirty-two million acres in the developing world. What biotech proponents fail to mention is that most of these "poor" farmers are in China and South Africa and grow Bt cotton, a nonfood crop. These farmers have to annually purchase the GE cotton by contract, as the seed companies forbid farmers from storing a part of the seed harvested for sowing in the next season. The question is how, in the long run, will these small-scale farmers be able to afford the purchase of transgenic seeds, which are more expensive than locally grown or conventional seeds? It remains to be seen whether, and for how long, Bt cotton's benefits for South African and Chinese farmers can be sustained against the emergence of pest resistance and in the face of unfavorable world markets. While industry proponents will often hold out the promise of 15 percent, 20 percent, or even 30 percent yield gains from biotechnology, smaller farms today produce from 200 to 1,000 percent more per unit area than larger farms worldwide (Rosset 1999). Land reforms that bring average land holdings down to their optimum (small) size from the inefficient, unproductive, overly large units that characterize much of world agriculture today, could provide the basis for production increases beside which the much ballyhooed promise of biotechnology would pale in comparison.

Most innovations in agricultural biotechnology have been profit-driven rather than need-driven. Biotechnological evolution is largely driven by decisions made by company investors who are preoccupied with corporate profitability and competitiveness, rather than the problems of poverty, food scarcity, and economic development in poor countries. The real thrust of the genetic engineering industry is not to make agriculture more productive, but rather to generate profits (Busch et al. 1990). This is illustrated by reviewing the principle technologies on the market today, which have been targeted toward the needs of large-scale commercial farmers, particularly in North America: (1) herbicide-resistant crops, such as Monsanto's "Roundup Ready" soybeans, seeds that are tolerant to Monsanto's herbicide "Roundup," and (2) "Bt" (*Bacillus thuringiensis*) crops, which are engineered to produce their own insecticide. In the first instance, the goal is to win greater herbicide market share for a proprietary product and in the second instance to boost seed sales—at the cost of damaging the usefulness of a key pest management product (the Bt-based microbial insecticide) relied upon by many farmers, including most organic farmers, as a powerful alternative to chemical insecticides.

These technologies respond to the need of biotechnology companies to intensify farmers' dependence upon seeds protected by so-called "intellectual property rights" (IPRs), which conflict directly with the age-old rights of farmers to reproduce, share, or store seeds (Fowler and Mooney 1990). Whenever possible, corporations require farmers to buy a company's brand of inputs and forbid farmers from keeping or selling seed. In the US, farmers adopting transgenic soybeans must sign an agreement with Monsanto. If they sow transgenic soybeans the next year, the penalty is about $3,000 per acre, depending on the acreage. This fine could cost farmers their farms, their livelihood. By controlling germplasm from seed to sale and by forcing farmers to pay inflated prices for seed-chemical packages, companies are determined to extract the most profit from their research investment (Krimsky and Wrubel 1996). Genetic engineering is attractive to firms because the ability to register exclusive ownership over new varieties makes it more feasible for them to recoup the high costs of biotechnology research and development.

The rapid accumulation of IPR over germplasm and enabling technologies has led to dramatic consolidation among biotech firms. This accumulation also hampers the exchange of data, plant material, and techniques among researchers in both public and private sectors. Largely in response to industry pressure, harmonized standards of IPR protection have been agreed upon at the global level (chiefly through the World Trade Organization's [WTO] TRIPS [trade-related aspects of intellectual property rights]) requiring developing countries to implement strong domestic IPR regimes. For the poorest countries, the cost of strong IPRs outweigh the benefits, as IPRs do little to stimulate investment in subsistence crops and traits relevant to poor farmers' food security.

Although India and China are constantly praised as examples of developing countries with very active plant biotechnology programs, most of the patents are held by Western corporations. These companies are trying to impose patenting on the rest of the world, which will ultimately give a handful of corporations full monopoly over genetic resources, limiting access to farmers who, in fact, have been the seed guardians for thousands of years.

WHAT ABOUT GOLDEN RICE?

Scientists who support biotechnology and disagree with the assertion that most biotechnology research is profit- rather than need-driven use the newly developed but not yet commercialized golden rice to hide behind a rhetoric of humanitarianism. This experimental rice is rich in beta-carotene, or vitamin A precursor, an important nutrient significant to millions of children—especially in Asia—who suffer from vitamin A deficiency, which can lead to blindness.

Developers of golden rice say that this new crop was developed with public funds and that, once the rice proves viable in field plantings, it will be freely distributed to the poor. The suggestion that genetically altered rice is the proper way to address the condition of two million children at risk of vitamin A deficiency–induced blindness reveals a tremendous naiveté about the reality and causes of vitamin and micronutrient malnutrition. Looking at the patterns of human development and nutrition, one must quickly realize that vitamin A deficiency is not best characterized as a problem but rather as a symptom, a warning sign. It warns us of broader inadequacies associated with both poverty and with agricultural change from diverse cropping systems toward rice monoculture promoted by the Green Revolution.

People do not exhibit vitamin A deficiency because rice contains too little vitamin A but rather because their diet has been reduced to rice and almost nothing else. They suffer from many other dietary illnesses that cannot be addressed by beta-carotene but could be addressed, together with vitamin A deficiency, by a more varied diet. Golden rice must be seen as a one-dimensional attempt to fix a problem created by the Green Revolution: the problem of diminished crop and dietary diversity.

A "magic bullet" solution, which places beta-carotene into rice—with potential health and ecological hazards—while leaving poverty, poor diets, and extensive monoculture intact, is unlikely to make any durable contribution to well-being. As Vandana Shiva has pointed out, "Such an approach reveals blindness to readily available solutions to vitamin A deficiency–induced blindness, including many ubiquitous leafy plants which when introduced (or re-introduced) into the diet provide both needed beta-carotene and other missing vitamins and micronutrients." Although wild green vegetables have been regarded as peripheral to the peasant household, gathering as currently practiced in many rural farming communities affords a meaningful addition to the peasant family nutrition and subsistence. Within and on the periphery of paddy rice fields there is an abundance of wild and cultivated green leafy vegetables rich in vitamins and nutrients, most of which are eliminated when farmers adopt monocultures and associated herbicides (Greenland 1997).

Rice biotechnologists have no understanding of the deeply rooted cultural traditions that determine food preferences among Asian people, especially the social and even religious significance of white rice. It is highly unlikely that golden rice will replace white rice, which for millennia has played a variety of nutritional, culinary, and ceremonial roles. There is no doubt that golden rice will collide with the traditions associated with white rice, as green or blue french fries would bump into food preferences in the United States. If golden rice is made for selected populations in Asia, it should be done without violating cultural practices, an aspect of the process about which corporations know very little.

Even if golden rice made it into the bowls of poor Asians, there is no guarantee that it would benefit poor people that don't eat fat-rich or oil-rich foods. Beta-carotene is fat-soluble, and its intake by the intestine depends upon fat or oil in the diet. Moreover, people suffering protein-related malnutrition and lacking dietary fats and oils cannot store vitamin A well in the liver, nor transport it to the different body tissues where the vitamin is needed. Given the low concentration of beta-carotene in golden rice, people would have to eat more than two pounds of rice per day to obtain the recommended daily allowance of vitamin A. Instead, less than half an ounce of a wild leafy vegetable usually eliminated by the herbicides associated with transgenic rice provides the recommended dosage.

An additional complication is that provitamin A in regular rice is lost if the grains are polished. Although many poor people do not polish their rice, thus benefiting from provitamin A present in the seed coat, many people cannot afford to grow rice, so they grow and eat barley instead.

DOES BIOTECHNOLOGY INCREASE YIELDS?

A major argument advanced by biotechnology proponents is that transgenic crops will significantly boost crop yields. These expectations have been examined by a US Department of Agriculture (USDA) Economic Research Service (ERS) report (1999), which analyzed data collected in 1997 and 1998 for twelve and eighteen US region/crop combinations, respectively. The crops surveyed were Bt corn and cotton, and herbicide-tolerant (HT) corn, cotton, and soybeans, and their nonengineered counterparts.

The yields in 1997 were not significantly different in engineered versus nonengineered crops in seven of twelve crop/region combinations. Four of twelve regions showed significant increases (13 to 21 percent) in yield of engineered versus nonengineered crops (HT soybeans in three regions and Bt cotton in one region). Herbicide-tolerant cotton in one region showed a significant reduction in yield (12 percent), compared with its nonengineered counterparts.

The yields in 1998 were not significantly different in engineered versus nonengineered crops in twelve of eighteen crop/region combinations. Five crop/region combinations (Bt corn in two regions, HT corn in one region, Bt cotton in two regions) showed significant increases in yield (5 to 30 percent) of genetically engineered over nonengineered crops, but only under high pressure from the European corn borer, which is sporadic. Herbicide-tolerant (glyphosate tolerant) cotton was the only engineered crop that showed no significant increase in yield in either region where it was surveyed. Based on a cross-sectional examination in 1998 of 365 crop fields in Iowa, GE crops provided farmers with no significant difference in economic returns. Yields from GE crops were slightly lower than yields from conventional varieties.

In 1999 researchers at the University of Nebraska's Institute of Agriculture and Natural Resources grew five different Monsanto soybean varieties, together with their closest conventional relatives, and the highest-yielding traditional varieties in four locations around the state using both drylands and irrigated fields. On average, researchers found the GE varieties—though more expensive—produced 6 percent less than their non–genetically engineered near relatives, and 11 percent less than the highest yielding conventional crops. Reports from Argentina show the same non–yield enhancing results with HT soybeans, which universally seems to exhibit yield drag. In fact, the yield penalty that accompanies the cultivation of herbicide-resistant crops can range up to 10 and 30 percent and is rarely factored into a farmer's calculations in advance. A review of 8,200 university-based trials revealed a mean yield loss of 4.6 bu/ac or 6.7 percent compared to top conventional trials. "Siren," the predominant triazine-resistant variety of canola grown in Australia throughout the 1990s, has a yield penalty of between 15 and 20 percent (Lurquin 2002).

Yield losses are amplified in crops, such as Bt corn, where it is mandatory for farmers to leave 20 percent of their land as refuges made up of nontransgenic corn. It is expected that patchworks of transgenic and nontransgenic crops can delay the evolution of pest resistance by providing susceptible insects harbored in the refuges for mating with resistant insects. The crops in the refuges are likely to sustain heavy damage and, thus, farmers incur yield losses. A refuge kept completely free of pesticides must be 20 to 30 percent the size of the engineered plot, but the refuge should be about 40 percent the size of the biotechnology plot if pesticides are to be used, since insecticide spraying can increase the odds of Bt resistance developing (Mellon and Rissler 1999).

If, instead, 30 percent of arable land was devoted

to growing soybeans in a strip cropping design (as many alternative farmers do in the Midwest), introducing potentials for internal rotation in the field and contour arrangements of strips to minimize erosion on hillsides, yields of up to 10 percent over comparable monocultures of corn and soybeans would be achieved (Ghaffaradeh et al. 1999). Moreover, European corn borers would be minimized, as pest populations tend to be lower in mixed and rotational cropping systems (Andow 1991).

In the case of cotton, there is no demonstrated need to introduce Bt toxin in the crop, as most Lepidoptera (butterfly and moth) species damaging this crop are pesticide-induced secondary pests. The best way to deal with them is not to spray insecticides, but instead use biological control or cultural techniques, such as rotation or strip-cropping with alfalfa. In the Southwest, the key pest is the boll weevil, a beetle immune to the Bt toxin.

DO TRANSGENIC CROPS REDUCE PESTICIDE USE?

Biotech supporters claim that an important benefit of bioengineered crops for farmers is the reduction of pesticide use. They state that adoption of Bt cotton in China has lowered the use of pesticides by 75 percent and reduced the number of pesticide poisonings an equivalent amount. In the Midwestern United States, despite all of the pressures for farmers to use insect resistant GE varieties, the benefits of using Bt corn are not assured because populations of the target pest, European corn borer, are not predictable. This pest reaches epidemic status every four to eight years. Given this unpredictability, it is not profitable for farmers to grow Bt corn when this insect is in low abundance. In fact, during the last five years, the percentage of field corn treated with insecticides in the United States has remained at approximately 30 percent despite a significant increase in the acres of Bt corn planted (Obrycki et al. 2001). Given the small acreage of corn treated with insecticides and the fact that insecticides are used mostly against root worms and soil insects, not European corn borer, at best, Bt corn could have reduced insecticide usage on 1 to 2 percent of the area (about 1.5 million acres) sown to corn in 1998, not the 15 million acres claimed by Monsanto and others. The reality is that assessments of changes in pesticide use are deficient. Even if a reduction in pesticide use may be observed, this cannot be used as a proxy for environmental benefits.

WHAT ARE THE COSTS TO AMERICAN FARMERS?

To assess farm economics and the impact of transgenic crops on United States farms, it is useful to examine the realities faced by Iowa farmers who live in the heartland of transgenic corn and soy. While weeds are an annoyance, the real problem the farmers face is falling farm prices, driven down by long-term overproduction. From 1990 to 1998, the average price of a metric ton of soybeans decreased 62 percent, and returns over nonland costs declined from $530 to $182 per hectare, a 66 percent drop. Faced with falling returns per hectare, farmers have had no choice but to "get big or get out." Only by increasing acreage to compensate for falling per-acre profits can farmers stay in business. Any technology that facilitates "getting big" will be seized upon, even if short-term gains are wiped out by prices that continue to fall as the industrial agricultural model expands.

For these Iowa farmers, reductions in return per unit of cropland have reinforced the importance of herbicides within the production process, as they reduce time devoted to mechanical cultivation and allow a given farmer to farm more acres. A survey of Iowa farmers conducted in 1998 indicated that the use of glyphosate with glyphosate-resistant soybean varieties reduced weed control costs by nearly 30 percent compared with conventional weed management for nontransgenic varieties. However, yields for the glyphosate-resistant soybeans were about 4 percent lower, and net returns per unit land area from glyphosate resistant and conventional soybeans were nearly identical (Duffy 1999).

From the standpoint of convenience and cost reduction, the use of broad-spectrum herbicides in combination with herbicide-resistant varieties appeals to farmers. Such systems fit well with large-scale operations, no-tillage production, and subcontracted chemical applications. However, from the standpoint of price, any penalty for transgenic varieties in the marketplace will make the impact of existing low prices even worse. Taking into account that American exports of soybeans to the European Union plummeted from eleven million to six million tons in 1999 due to rejection of GMOs by European consumers, it is easy to predict disaster for farmers dependent on transgenic crops. Durable solutions to the dilemmas facing Iowa farmers will not come from herbicide-tolerant crops, but from a fundamental restructuring of Midwestern agriculture (Brummer 1998).

The integration of the seed and chemical industries appears to accelerate increases in per-acre expenditures for seeds plus chemicals, delivering significantly lower returns to growers. Companies developing herbicide-tolerant crops are trying to shift as much per-acre cost as possible from the herbicide onto the seed-by-seed costs and technology charges. Increasingly, price reductions for herbicides will be limited to growers purchasing technology packages. In Illinois, the adoption of herbicide-resistant crops makes for the most expensive soybean seed-plus-weed management system in modern history—between $40 and $60 per acre depending on fee rates, weed pressure, and so on. Three years ago, the average seed-plus-weed control costs on Illinois farms was $26 per acre and represented 23 percent of variable costs. Today, they represent 35 to 40 percent (Carpenter and Gianessi 1999). Farmers may experience significant savings in herbicide costs (up to 30 percent) but the difference is in seed cost. In 1998, Iowa farmers spent $26.42 per acre on GE seeds while the cost of conventional seed was only $18.89 per acre. Many farmers are willing to pay for the simplicity and robustness of the new weed management system, but such advantages may be short-lived as ecological problems arise.

But as emphasized before, the ultimate cost that farmers pay is their increased dependence on the biotechnological inputs protected by a ruthless system of intellectual property rights that legally inhibits the right of farmers to reproduce, share, and store seed (Busch et al. 1990). Farmers who exert this right by breaking the signed contract with a corporation stand to lose their farms.

WILL BIOTECHNOLOGY BENEFIT POOR FARMERS?

Most biotechnological innovations available today bypass poor farmers, as these farmers are not able to afford the seeds, which are protected by patents owned by biotech corporations. Extending modern technology to resource-poor farmers has been historically constrained by considerable environmental obstacles. An estimated 850 million people live on land threatened by desertification; another 500 million reside on terrain that is too steep to cultivate. Because of these and other limitations, about two million people have been untouched by modern agricultural science. Most of the rural poor live in the latitudes between the Tropic of Cancer and the Tropic of Capricorn, a region that is the most vulnerable to the effects of global warming. In such environments, a plethora of cheap and locally accessible technologies must be available to enhance rather than limit farmers' options, a trend that corporate-controlled biotechnology inhibits.

Biotech researchers pledge to counter problems associated with food production in such marginal areas by developing GMO crops with traits considered desirable by small farmers, such as enhanced competitiveness against weeds and drought tolerance. However, these new attributes would not necessarily be a panacea. Traits such as drought tolerance are polygenic —determined by the interaction of multiple genes. Consequently, the development of crops with such traits is a complex process that could take at least ten years and is not in the agenda of companies interested in recovering the high cost of biotech research and development.

Under these circumstances, genetic engineering does not give something for nothing. When we tinker with multiple genes to create a desired trait, we inevitably end up sacrificing other traits, such as productivity. As a result, use of a drought-tolerant plant would boost crop yields by only 10 to 30 percent. Any additional yield increases would have to come from improved environmental practices (such as water harvesting or enhancing soil organic matter for improved moisture retention) rather than from the genetic manipulation of specific characteristics (Persley and Lantin 2000).

Even if biotechnology could contribute to increased crop harvests, poverty will not necessarily decline. Many poor farmers in developing countries do not have access to cash, credit, technical assistance, or markets. The so-called Green Revolution of the 1950s and 1960s bypassed such farmers because planting the new high-yield crops and maintaining them through the use of pesticides and fertilizers was too costly for impoverished landowners. Data shows that in both Asia and Latin America, wealthy farmers with larger and better-endowed lands gained the most from the Green Revolution, where farmers with fewer resources often gained little (Lappé, Collins et al. 1998). The "Gene Revolution" might only end up repeating the mistakes of its predecessor. Genetically modified seeds are under corporate control and patent protection, consequently making them very expensive. Since many developing countries still lack the institutional infrastructure and low-interest credit necessary to deliver these new seeds to poor farmers, biotechnology will only exacerbate marginalization.

Poor farmers do not fit into the marketing niche of

private corporations, which focus on biotechnological innovations for the commercial-agricultural sectors of industrial and developing nations; this is where these corporations can expect a huge return on their research investment. The private sector often ignores important crops such as cassava, which is a staple for 500 million people worldwide. The few impoverished landowners with access to biotechnology will become dangerously dependent on the annual purchase of genetically modified seeds. These farmers will have to abide by onerous intellectual property agreements not to plant seeds yielded from a harvest of genetically engineered plants. Such stipulations are an affront to traditional farmers, who for centuries have saved and shared seeds as part of their cultural legacy (Kloppenburg 1998).

Some scientists and policy makers suggest that large investments through public-private partnerships can help developing countries acquire the indigenous scientific and institutional capacity to shape biotechnology to suit the needs and circumstances of small farmers. But once again, corporate intellectual property rights to genes and gene-cloning technology are likely to play spoiler. For instance, Brazil's national research institute (EMBRAPA) has to negotiate license agreements with nine different companies before a virus-resistant papaya developed with researchers at Cornell University can be released to poor farmers (Persley and Lantin 2000). It is not clear how the soon to be commercialized varieties of insect-resistant rice for Asia, virus-resistant sweet potato for Africa, and virus-resistant papaya for Caribbean nations will be released by national institutions in the face of the patent limitations encountered by the Brazilian institute.

THE IMPLICATIONS OF GENETIC POLLUTION OF NATIVE VARIETIES VIA TRANSGENIC CROPS

Concerns have been raised about whether the introduction of transgenic crops may replicate or further aggravate the effects of the Green Revolution miracle varieties on the genetic diversity of landraces and wild relatives in areas of crop origin and diversification and, therefore, affecting the cultural thread of peasant communities. The debate was prompted by *Nature*'s controversial article reporting the presence of introgressed transgenic DNA constructs in native maize landraces grown in remote mountains in Oaxaca, Mexico (Quist and Chapela 2001). Although there is a high probability that the introduction of transgenic crops will further accelerate the loss of genetic diversity and of indigenous knowledge and culture through mechanisms similar to those of the Green Revolution, there are some fundamental differences in the magnitude of the impacts. The Green Revolution increased the rate at which modern varieties replaced folk varieties, without necessarily changing the genetic integrity of local varieties. Genetic erosion involves a loss of local varieties, but it can be slowed and even reversed through in situ conservation efforts that conserve not only land-races and wild-weedy relatives, but also agroecological and cultural relationships of crop evolution and management in specific localities.

The problem with introductions of transgenic crops into diversity regions is that the spread of characteristics of genetically altered grain to local varieties favored by small farmers could dilute the natural sustainability of these races. Proponents of biotechnology believe that unwanted gene flow from GM maize may not compromise maize biodiversity (and therefore the associated systems of agricultural knowledge and practice along with the ecological and evolutionary processes involved) and may pose no worse a threat than cross-pollination from conventional (non-GM) seed. In fact, some industry researchers believe that DNA from engineered maize is unlikely to have an evolutionary advantage, but if transgenes do persist they may actually prove advantageous to Mexican farmers and crop diversity. However, here a key question arises: Can genetically engineered plants actually increase crop production and, at the same time, repel pests, resist herbicides, and confer adaptation to stressful factors commonly faced by small farmers? Thermodynamic considerations suggest they cannot; traits important to indigenous farmers (resistance to drought, food or fodder quality, maturity, competitive ability, performance on intercrops, storage quality, taste or cooking properties, compatibility with household labor conditions, etc.) could be traded for transgenic qualities that may not be important to farmers (Jordon 2001). In other words, by expressing a new trait such as herbicide resistance, local varieties may lose traits such as drought resistance that are key to poor farmers. Under this scenario risk will increase and farmers will lose their ability to adapt to changing biophysical environments and be unable to produce relatively stable yields with a minimum of external inputs while supporting community food security.

As conversion from subsistence to cash agricultural economy occurs, the loss of biodiversity in many rural societies is progressing at an alarming rate. As peasants directly link to the market economy, economic forces increasingly influence the mode of production characterized by genetically uniform crops and mechanized or agrochemical packages. As adoption of modern varieties occurs, landraces and wild relatives are progressively abandoned, becoming relics or extinct.

These trends are expected to be aggravated by the technological evolution of agriculture based on emerging biotechnologies whose development and commercialization is increasingly concentrated and under the control of a few corporations, accompanied by the increased withdrawal of the public sector as major provider of research and extension services to rural communities (Jordan 2001). The social impacts of local crop shortfalls, resulting from genetic uniformity or changes in the genetic integrity of local varieties due to genetic pollution, can be considerable in the margins of the developing world. In the extreme periphery, crop losses mean ongoing ecological degradation, poverty, hunger, and even famine. It is under these conditions of systemic market failures and lack of public external assistance that local skills and resources associated with biological and cultural diversity should be preserved and made available to rural populations to maintain or recover their production processes.

Diverse agricultural systems and genetic materials that confer high levels of tolerance to changing socioeconomic and environmental conditions are extremely valuable to poor farmers, as diverse systems buffer against natural or human-induced variations in production conditions (Altieri 1996). It is crucial that impoverished rural populations maintain low-risk agroecosystems that are primarily structured to ensure local food security. Farmers in the margins must continue to produce food for their local communities in the absence of modern inputs, and this can be reached by preserving in situ ecologically intact locally adapted agrobiodiversity. For this, it will be necessary to maintain pools of genetically diverse material, geographically isolated from any possibility of cross-fertilization or genetic pollution from uniform transgenic crops. These islands of traditional germplasm within specific agroecological landscapes will act as extant safeguards against the potential ecological failure derived from the second Green Revolution imposed in the margins.

The above concerns about gene flow from transgenic crops are also relevant in the US, where a recent report noted contamination (between 50 and 80 percent of the samples) of the seed supply of conventional maize, soybean, and canola by DNA sequences from transgenic varieties of the same crops (Mellon and Rissler 2004).

CHAPTER TWO

Genetically Modified Crops and Human Health

ARE TRANSGENIC CROPS SIMILAR TO CONVENTIONALLY BRED CROPS?

US government regulatory agencies consider crops bred through biotechnology and conventional plant breeding to be "substantially equivalent." This presumption is profoundly flawed and scientifically unsupported. Most evidence shows that gene transfer using rDNA techniques is substantially different from the processes that govern gene transfer in traditional breeding. In the latter endeavor, plant breeders develop new varieties through the process of selection and seek to achieve expression of genetic material that is already present within a species. Conventional crossing involves the movement of clusters of functionally linked genes, primarily between similar chromosomes, and includes the relevant promoters, regulatory sequences, and associated genes involved in the coordinated expression of the character of interest in the plant.

Genetic engineering works primarily through insertion of genetic material that is usually from unprecedented sources—genetic material from species, families, and even kingdoms which could not previously be sources of genetic material for a particular species. The process involves a "gene gun," a "promoter" gene from a virus, and a marker as a part of the package or construct inserted into the host plant cell. Current rDNA technologies involve the random insertion of genes in the absence of normal promoter sequences and associated regulatory genes. As there are very few examples of plant traits in which the associated regulatory genes have been identified, the introduction of a fully "functional" gene using rDNA techniques is currently not possible. The rDNA techniques involve the simultaneous insertion of viral promoters and selectable markers, and facilitate the introduction of genes from incompatible species; these genetic transformations cannot occur using traditional approaches, further illustrating the profound manner in which these two processes differ (Hansen 1999).

In summary, genetic engineering clearly differs from conventional breeding, which relies primarily on selection, using a natural process of sexual or asexual reproduction within a species or within closely related genera. Genetic engineering utilizes a process of insertion of genetic material, via a gene gun or a special bacterial truck that does not occur in nature. Biotechnologists can insert genetic material from any life-form into any other, attempting to create novel organisms with which there is no evolutionary experience. Biotechnologists argue that plant breeding has been going on since the beginning of agriculture and that every crop is a product of repeated genetic editing by humans over the past few millennia. To a certain degree this is true, but splicing bacterial genes into corn and carrots is not exactly what Neolithic civilizations could have done. Many aspects of plant biotechnology are different and have nothing to do with the way farmers breed crops or with conventional breeding. Had this been admitted earlier by biotechnologists perhaps certain aspects of the GMO debate would not be so polarized.

ARE TRANSGENIC CROPS SAFE TO EAT?

The premature commercial release of transgenic crops due to commercial pressures and lax FDA and EPA policies (condoning GE crops as "substantially equivalent" to conventional crops) has occurred in the context of a regulatory framework that seems inadequate, nontransparent, and, in some cases, completely absent. In fact, approval for commercial release of transgenic crops is based on scientific information provided voluntarily by companies producing GE crops.

It is estimated that about 50 percent of the corn- and soybean-based food in the US comes from GE corn and soybeans. Most consumers are not aware of this and have no possibility of identifying transgenic food not labeled as such. Given the fact that no scientist can ascertain that such foods are completely risk-free, it appears that the majority of the US population is being subjected to a large-scale feeding experiment. Consumers in the European Union (EU) have rejected such GMO foods (Lappé and Bailey 1998).

Because of the unusual methods used to breed GE crops, some fear that the genetic variants produced could introduce foreign substances into the food supply with unanticipated negative effects on human health. When food crops are genetically modified one or more genes are incorporated into the food crop's genome, using a vector containing several genes such as viral promoters, transcription terminators, antibiotic resistance markers, and reporter genes. Data on the safety of these are scarce despite the fact that DNA does not always fully break down in the alimentary tract. Gut bacteria can take up gene and GM plasmids, and this opens up the possibility of the spread of antibiotic resistance.

One major concern is the small but real chance that genetic engineering may transfer new and unidentified proteins into food, triggering allergic reactions in millions of consumers who are sensitive to allergens and have no way of identifying or protecting themselves from offending foods (Burks and Fuchs 1995).

Biotechnology introduces genes into various plants that are sources of food and food components. Introduced traits include insect and virus resistance, herbicide tolerance, and changes in composition or nutritional content. Given such a diversity of traits, there is a potential for allergenic proteins to be introduced into foods from sources with no history of having allergens or that have amino acid sequence similarities to known food allergens. When the gene comes from a crop, it is easy to establish if the GM food is allergenic using in-vitro tests. Assessment of the allergenicity is difficult when the gene is transferred from a source not eaten before or with unknown allergic properties. Presently, only indirect methods, such as finding SHORT sequence homologous to about 200 known allergens, are used for the assessment of allergenicity. In the absence of reliable methods it is, at present, impossible to definitely establish whether a new GM crop is allergenic or not before it is released into the human food chain.

Another concern is associated with the antibiotic resistance genes incorporated into nearly every GM crop plant as markers to indicate that a plant has been successfully engineered. These genes and their enzyme products, which cause antibiotics to be deactivated, are expected to be present in GE foods, raising important questions about the implications for human health, particularly in regard to compromising human immunity (Ticciati and Ticciati 1998).

FlavrSavr™ tomatoes contained a bacterial gene coding for resistance to the antibiotic Kamamycin. If one were treated with Kamamycin for an infection, and if one had eaten a FlavrSavr™ tomato in a salad for lunch, the enzyme responsible for Kamamycin inactivation would be present in one's body. Companies are announcing techniques to breed out antibiotic resistance and to stop using antibiotic resistance markers altogether. This is obviously a positive step, but one wonders if there may be long-term effects associated with past consumption of these products that may become obvious after a few years or in the presence of new pathogens.

Genetic engineering may remove or deactivate valuable nutritional substances in food. Recent research shows that GE herbicide-resistant soybeans have lower levels (12 to 14 percent) of isoflavones, key phytoestrogens (mostly genistin) that occur naturally in soybeans and may protect women from severe forms of cancer (Lappé, Bailey et al. 1999). Moreover, because of human error somewhere along the food chain from producer to consumer, foodstuff contamination with unauthorized genetically altered products increases with each step. This is what happened in October 2000 in several western US states where taco and tostada shells made from corn revealed the presence of a Cry9C

Bt toxin variant that had not been approved by the Food and Drug Administration (FDA) for human consumption. It is thought that the presence of unapproved genetically modified corn in taco shells was due to unintentional contamination of regular corn with StarLink™, a Bt variety used only for animal feed.

In summary, no scientist can negate the possibility that changing the fundamental genetic makeup of a food could cause new diseases or health problems. No long-term studies prove the safety of GM crops. These products are not being thoroughly tested before they arrive on the grocery shelves. Rather, they are being tested on consumers.

CHAPTER THREE

Biotechnology, Agriculture, and the Environment

MONOCULTURES AND THE DANGER OF GENETIC EROSION

Biotechnology is being pursued to repair the problems (pesticide resistance, pollution, soil degradation, etc.) caused by previous agrochemical technologies promoted by the same companies now leading the biorevolution. Transgenic crops developed for pest control closely follow the paradigm of using a single control mechanism (a pesticide) that has proven to fail repeatedly with insects, pathogens, and weeds (national Research Council 1996). The touted "one gene–one pest" approach can be easily overcome by pests that are continuously adapting to new situations and evolving detoxification mechanisms (Robinson 1996).

Agricultural systems developed with transgenic crops favor monocultures characterized by dangerously high levels of genetic homogeneity, leading to higher vulnerability of agricultural systems to biotic and abiotic stresses (Robinson 1996). There have been cases in history (i.e., the Irish potato famine, French wine industry, corn production in the US Midwest) of entire crops wiped out by disease because of the narrow genetic diversity of crops planted over large areas. Planting GE crops repeats past historical mistakes: Large stands of one crop variety are planted, supplanting all others, making the one dominant variety profoundly vulnerable. Current monocultural practices associated with GE crops are further narrowing the gene pool until it can no longer prevent a catastrophic epidemic. By promoting monocultures, biotechnology also undermines ecological methods of farming, such as rotation and multicropping, exacerbating the problems of conventional agriculture (Altieri 2000).

As new GE seeds replace the old traditional varieties and their wild relatives, genetic erosion will accelerate in the developing world (Fowler and Mooney 1990). The push for uniformity will not only destroy the diversity of genetic resources, but also disrupt the biological complexity that underlies the sustainability of indigenous farming systems (Altieri 1996).

There are many unanswered ecological questions

regarding the impact of releasing transgenic plants and microorganisms into the environment, and the available evidence supports the proposition that the impact can be substantial. Among the major environmental risks associated with genetically engineered plants are the unintended transfer to plant relatives of "transgenes" with unpredictable ecological effects (Rissler and Mellon 1996).

HERBICIDE RESISTANCE

By creating crops resistant to its herbicides, a biotech company can expand markets for its patented chemicals. (In 1997, 50,000 farmers grew almost nine million acres of herbicide-resistant soybeans, equivalent to 13 percent of the seventy-one million acres of soybeans in the US.) Observers gave a value of $75 million for herbicide-resistant crops in 1995, the first year they were marketed, indicating that by the year 2000 the market would be approximately $805 million, representing a 61 percent growth (Carpenter and Gianessi 1999). Globally, in 2002, herbicide-resistant soybean occupied over ninety million acres, making it by far the number one GE crop in terms of area.

The continuous use of herbicides such as bromoxynil and glyphosate (also known as "Roundup," by Monsanto), which herbicide-resistant crops tolerate, can lead to problems (Goldberg 1992). It is well documented that when a single herbicide is used repeatedly on a crop, the chances of herbicide resistance developing in weed populations greatly increases (Holt et al. 1993). About 216 cases of pesticide resistance have been reported in one or more herbicide chemical families (Holt and Le Baron 1990). Triazine herbicides are associated with the most resistant weed species (about sixty).

Given industry pressures to increase herbicide sales, acreage treated with broad-spectrum herbicides will expand, exacerbating the resistance problem. For example, it has been projected that the acreage treated with glyphosate will expand to nearly 150 million acres. Although glyphosate is considered less prone to weed resistance, the increased use of this herbicide will result in weed resistance, even if more slowly. This has already been documented with Australian populations of annual ryegrass, quackgrass, birdsfoot trefoil, Cirsium arvense, and Eleusine indica (Altieri 2000a).

Herbicide resistance becomes more of a problem as the number of herbicide modes of action to which weeds are exposed become fewer and fewer, a trend that herbicide-tolerant (HT) crops reinforce due to market forces. In fact, weed populations develop that can tolerate or "avoid" certain herbicides, such as the case in Iowa where common waterhemp populations demonstrated delayed germination and have "avoided" planned glyphosate applications. The GE crop itself may also assume weed status in crops that follow. For example, in Canada, volunteer canola resistant to three herbicides (glyphosate, imidazolinone, and glufosino-late) has been detected, a case of "stacked" or "multi-ple" resistance.

HERBICIDES KILL MORE THAN WEEDS

Biotech companies claim that when properly applied herbicides should not pose negative effects on humans or the environment. Large scale cropping of GE crops encourages aerial application of herbicides, and much of what is sprayed is wasted through drift, poisoning soil microorganisms such as mycorrhizal fungi—and even earthworms. But companies contend that bro-moxynil and glyphosate degrade rapidly in the soil, do not accumulate in ground water, have no effects on nontarget organisms, and leave no residue in foods. However, there is evidence that bromoxynil causes birth defects in laboratory animals, is toxic to fish, and may cause cancer in humans (Goldberg 1992). Because bromoxynil is absorbed through the skin, it is also likely to pose hazards to farmers and farmworkers. Similarly, glyphosate has been reported to be toxic to some nontarget species in the soil—both to beneficial predators such as spiders, mites, and carabid and coc-cinellid beetles, and to detritivores such as earthworms, as well as to aquatic organisms, including fish (Paoletti and Pimentel 1996). Glyphosate is a systemic herbi-cide (it moves through the plant phloem) and is carried into the harvested parts of plants. Exactly how much glyphosate is present in the seeds of HT corn or soybeans is not known, as grain products are not included in conventional market surveys for pesticide residues. The fact that this and other herbicides are known to accumulate in fruits and tubers (because they suffer little metabolic degradation in plants) raises questions about food safety, especially now that more than thirty-seven million pounds of this herbicide are used annually in the United States alone.

Even in the absence of immediate (acute) effects, it might take forty years for a potential carcinogen to act in enough people for it to be detected as a cause. Moreover, research has shown that glyphosate seems to act in a similar fashion to antibiotics by altering soil biology in a yet unknown way and causing effects such as

- Reducing the ability of soybeans and clover to fix nitrogen
- Rendering bean plants more vulnerable to disease
- Reducing growth of beneficial soil-dwelling mycorrhizal fungi, which are key for helping plants extract phosphorous from the soil.

In the farm-scale evaluations of HT crops recently completed in the United Kingdom (Firbank 2003), researchers showed that reduction of weed biomass, flowering, and seeding parts under HT crop management within and in margins of beet and spring oilseed rape involved changes in insect resource availability with knock-on effects, resulting in abundance reduction of several true bugs, butterflies, and bees. Counts of predacious carabid beetles that feed on weed seeds were also smaller in HT crop fields. The abundance of invertebrates that are food for mammals, birds, and other invertebrates were also found to be generally lower in HT beet and oilseed rape. The absence of flowering weeds in such GE fields can have serious consequences for beneficial insects (pest predators and parasitoids), which require pollen and nectar for survival and optimal efficiency.

CREATION OF "SUPERWEEDS"

Although there is some concern that transgenic crops might themselves become weeds, the major ecological risk is that large-scale releases of transgenic crops may promote transfer of transgenes from crops to other plants, which then could become weeds (Darmancy 1994). Transgenes that confer significant biological advantage may transform wild/weedy plants into new or more invasive weeds (Rissler and Mellon 1996). The biological process of concern here is introgression— hybridization among distinct plant species. Evidence indicates that such genetic exchanges among wild, weed, and crop plants have already occurred. The incidence of shattercane (*Sorghum bicolor*), a weedy relative of sorghum, and the gene flows between maize and teosinte (*Euchlaena mexicana,* a fodder plant) demonstrate the potential for crop relatives to become serious weeds. This is worrisome given that a number of US crops are grown in close proximity to sexually compatible wild relatives (Lutman 1999). Extreme care should be taken in plant systems exhibiting easy cross-pollination, such as oats, barley, sunflowers, and wild relatives, and between rapeseed and related crucifers (Snow and Moran 1997). Gene exchanges pose major threats to centers of diversity; in biodiverse farming systems the probability for transgenic crops of finding sexually compatible wild relatives is very high.

In Europe, there is a major concern about the possibility of pollen transfer of herbicide-tolerant genes from *Brassica* oilseeds to *Brassica nigra* and *Sinapis arvensis* (Casper and Landsmann 1992). There are also crops that are grown near wild weedy plants that are not close relatives but may have some degree of cross-compatibility, such as the crosses of *Raphanus raphanistrum* x *R. sativus* (radish) and Johnson grass x sorghum corn (Radosevich et al. 1996). Cascading repercussions of these transfers may ultimately mean changes in the makeup of plant communities.

The transfer of genes from transgenic crops to organically grown crops poses a specific problem to organic farmers. Organic certification depends on the growers' being able to guarantee that their crops have no inserted genes. Crops able to outbreed, such as maize or oilseed rape, will be affected to the greatest extent, but all organic farmers are at risk of genetic contamination. There are no regulations that enforce minimum isolating distances between transgenic and organic fields (Royal Society 1998).

Interspecific hybridization and introgression are common to species such as sunflower, maize, sorghum, oilseed rape, rice, wheat, and potatoes, providing a basis to expect gene flow between transgenic crops and wild relatives to create new herbicide-resistant weeds (Lutman 1999). There is consensus among scientists that transgenic crops will eventually allow transgenes to escape into free living populations of wild relatives. The disagreements lie in how serious the impact will be from such transfers (Snow and Moran 1997).

CHAPTER FOUR

Environmental Risks of Insect-Resistant Crops (Bt Crops)

RESISTANCE

The biotech industry promises that transgenic crops inserted with Bt genes will no longer need the synthetic insecticides now used to control insect pests. But how this will happen is not so clear; most crops have a diversity of insect pests and insecticides will still have to be applied to control nonlepidopteran pests, which are not susceptible to the Bt toxin expressed by the crop (Gould 1994). In fact, in a recent report (USDA 1999) an analysis of pesticide use in the 1997 US growing season in twelve region/crop combinations showed that in seven sites there was no statistically significant difference in pesticide use on Bt crops versus non-Bt crops. In the Mississippi Delta, significantly more pesticides were used on Bt versus non-Bt cotton.

On the other hand, several lepidopteran species have been reported to develop resistance to Bt toxin in both field and laboratory tests, suggesting that major resistance problems are likely to develop in Bt crops, which through the continuous expression of the toxin create a strong selection pressure (Tabashnik 1994). No serious entomologist questions whether resistance will develop or not. The question is, how fast? Scientists have already detected development of "behavioral resistance" by some insects that take advantage of the uneven expression of toxin potency within crop foliage, attacking tissue patches with low toxin concentrations. As genetically inserted toxins often decrease in leaf and stem tissues as crops reach maturation, the low dose can only kill or debilitate completely susceptible larvae (homozygotes); consequently, adaptation to the Bt toxin can occur much faster if the concentration always remains high. Observation of transgenic corn plants in late October indicated that most European corn borers who survived had entered dormancy in preparation for emergence in the following spring as adults (Onstad and Gould 1998). Arizona researchers found in 1997 that approximately 3.2 percent of pink bollworm larvae collected from cotton fields exhibited resistance. This level was far above what was expected.

In order to delay the inevitable development of

resistance by insects to Bt crops, bioengineers are preparing resistance management plans, which consist of patchworks of transgenic and nontransgenic crops (called refuges) to delay the evolution of resistance by providing susceptible insects for mating with resistant insects. Although the size of refuges should be at least 30 percent of the crop area, according to members of the Campaign for Food Safety, Monsanto's new plan calls for only 20 percent refuges, even when insecticides are to be used. Moreover, the plan offers no details whether the refuges must be planted alongside the transgenic crops or some distance away, where studies suggest they would be less effective (Mallet and Porter 1992). In addition to refuges requiring the difficult goal of regional coordination between farmers, it is unrealistic to expect most farmers with small and medium-sized farms to devote up to 30 to 40 percent of their crop area to refuges, especially if crops in these areas are to sustain heavy pest damage.

This strategy to counter development of resistance is now threatened by gene flow from Bt maize and Bt cotton (which grew on more than 14 million hectares worldwide in 2002), which could cause Bt toxin production in seeds of refuge plants. Such refuge contamination has already been detected in Texas and is bound to affect major pests such as the cotton pink bollworm, the corn earworm, and the European corn-borer (Chilcutt and Tabashnik 2004).

The farmers that face the greatest risk from the

development of insect resistance to Bt are neighboring organic farmers who grow corn and soybeans without agrochemicals. Once resistance appears in insect populations, organic farmers will not be able to use *Bacillus thuringiensis* in its microbial insecticide form to control the lepidopteran pests that move in from adjacent neighboring transgenic fields. In addition, genetic pollution of organic crops resulting from gene flow (pollen) from transgenic crops can jeopardize the certification of organic crops and organic farmers may lose premium markets. Who will compensate these farmers for such losses?

We know from the history of agriculture that plant diseases, insect pests, and weeds become more severe with the development of monocultures, and that intensively managed and genetically manipulated crops soon lose genetic diversity (Altieri 1994; Robinson 1996). Based on the fact that more than 500 species of pests have already evolved resistance to conventional insecticides, surely pests can also evolve resistance to Bt toxins in transgenic crops. Therefore there is no reason to believe that resistance to transgenic crops will not evolve among insects, weeds, and pathogens, as has happened with pesticides. No matter what resistance management strategies will be used, pests will adapt and overcome the agronomic constraints (Green 1990). Studies of pesticide resistance demonstrate that unintended selection can result in pest problems greater than those that existed before deployment of new insecticides. Diseases and pests have always been amplified by changes toward genetically homogenous agriculture, precisely the type of farming that biotechnology promotes (Robinson 1996). A better approach would be to design technologies to increase tolerance to pests rather than resistance to pests. Tolerance does not rely on toxicity to kill pests, is not eroded by resistance in pest populations, and does not negatively impact nontarget organisms.

EFFECTS ON NONTARGET SPECIES

By keeping pest populations at extremely low levels, Bt crops could potentially starve natural enemies; the predators and parasitic wasps that feed on pests need a small amount of prey to survive in the agroecosystem. Among the natural enemies that live exclusively on insects which the transgenic crops are designed to kill (Lepidoptera), egg and larval parasitoids would be most affected because they are totally dependant on live hosts for development and survival, though some predators could theoretically thrive on dead or dying prey (Schuler et al. 1999).

Natural enemies could also be affected directly through intertrophic level effects of the toxin. The potential of Bt toxins moving through insect food chains poses serious implications for natural biocontrol in agricultural fields. Recent evidence shows that the Bt toxin can affect beneficial insect predators that feed on insect pests present on Bt crops (Hilbeck et al. 1998). Studies in Switzerland show that the mean total mortality of predaceous lacewing larvae (Chrysopidae) raised on Bt-fed prey was 62 percent compared to 37 percent when raised on Bt-free prey. The Bt prey–fed Chrysopidae also exhibited prolonged development time throughout their immature life stage (Hilbeck et al. 1998). In this study, reduced prey quality is likely to have contributed to the negative effects on the lacewing. The sublethal effect shows the scope for the fitness of natural enemies to be indirectly affected by Bt toxins exposed to GE crops via feeding on suboptimal food or because of host death and scarcity. Moreover, the toxins produced by Bt plants may be passed on to predators and parasitoids via pollen. No one has analyzed the consequences of such transfers on the myriad of natural enemies that depend on pollen for reproduction and longevity.

These findings are of concern to small farmers who rely on the rich complex of predators and parasites associated with their mixed cropping systems for insect pest control (Altieri 1994). Intertrophic level effects of the Bt toxin raise serious concerns about the potential of the disruption of natural pest control. Polyphagous predators that move within and between mixed crops/cultivars will encounter Bt-containing nontarget prey throughout the crop season (Hilbeck et al. 1999). Disrupted biocontrol mechanisms may result in increased crop losses due to pests or to increased use of pesticide by farmers, with consequent health and environmental hazards.

It is also now known that windblown pollen from Bt crops found on natural vegetation surrounding transgenic fields can kill nontarget insects. A Cornell University study (Losey et al. 1999) showed that corn pollen containing Bt toxin can drift several meters downwind and deposit itself on milkweed foliage with potentially damaging effects on monarch butterfly populations. These findings open a whole new dimension on the unexpected impacts of transgenic crops on nontarget organisms that play key and many times unknown roles in the ecosystem.

EFFECTS ON THE SOIL ECOSYSTEM

The environmental effects of Bt crops are not limited to crops and insects. Bt toxins can be incorporated into the soil though leaf materials when farmers plow under transgenic crop residues after harvest. Toxins may persist for two to three months, resisting degradation by binding to clay and humic acid soil particles, while maintaining toxin activity (Palm et al. 1996). Such active Bt toxins that end up and accumulate in the soil and water from transgenic leaf litter may have negative impacts on soil and aquatic invertebrates and nutrient cycling processes (Donnegan and Seidler 1999). Researchers have found that 25 to 30 percent of the Cry1A proteins produced by Bt cotton leaves remain bound in the soil even after 140 days. In a recent study, after 200 days of exposure, adult earthworms experienced a significant weight loss when fed Bt corn litter compared with earthworms fed non-Bt corn litter.

Other investigations confirm the fact that Bt retains its insecticidal properties and is protected against microbial degradation by being bound to soil particles, persisting in various soils for at least 234 days. If transgenic crops substantially alter soil biota and affect processes such as soil organic matter decomposition and mineralization, this would be of serious concern for poor farmers who cannot purchase expensive chemical fertilizers. These farmers instead rely on local residues, organic matter, and soil microorganisms (key invertebrate, fungal, or bacterial species) for soil fertility, which can be negatively affected by the soil-bound toxin (Saxena et al. 1999).

A PRECAUTIONARY TALE

The ecological effects of genetically engineered crops are not limited to pest resistance and the creation of new weeds or virus strains. As argued previously, transgenic crops can produce environmental toxins that move through the food chain and also may end up in the soil and water, affecting invertebrates and probably ecological processes such as nutrient cycling. Moreover, the large-scale landscape homogenization with transgenic crops will exacerbate the ecological vulnerability already associated with monoculture agriculture (Altieri 2000). Unquestioned expansion of this technology into developing countries is not desirable. The strength inherent in the agricultural diversity of many of these countries would be inhibited or reduced by extensive monoculture; the consequences will result in serious social and environmental problems (Thrupp 1998).

Despite these concerns, transgenic crops have been rushed into international markets and are massively deployed in the agricultural landscapes of the USA, Canada, Argentina, China, and other countries, where over half of the area planted to major crops such as soybean, corn, and canola is occupied by transgenic varieties. It is unfortunate that only now, after four years of massive commercial use of transgenic crops, former US Secretary of Agriculture Dan Glickman has called for studies to assess the long-term ecological and health effects of these crops. This comes a bit late, given that the ecological release of genes is nonretrievable and their effects irreversible. On top of this, a very small fraction, 3 percent or less, of biotechnology budgets are spent on biosafety or biodiversity studies, and key long-term ecological experiments on environmental risks of GE crops are still sorely lacking.

The rapid release of transgenic crops and the ensuing financial disarray (share prices for biotechnology companies are sinking to all-time lows) are disturbingly reminiscent of the earlier uncritical bandwagons for nuclear energy and chlorinated pesticides such as DDT. A combination of public opposition and financial liability eventually forced retrenchment of these earlier technologies; their effects on the environment and human health proved to be far more complex, diffuse, and lingering than the promises that accompanied their rapid commercialization. In many cases chronic environmental and health effects were not noticed until decades after their release. Repeated use of transgenic crops in an area may result in cumulative effects such as those resulting from the buildup of toxins in soils. For this reason, risk assessment studies not only have to be of an ecological nature in order to capture effects on ecosystem processes, but also must be of sufficient duration so that probable accumulative effects can be detected. A decade of careful ecological monitoring of field and larger scale study results are necessary to assess the full potential for GM crops' risk to the environment. The application of multiple diagnostic methods to assess multitrophic effects and impacts on agroecosystem function will provide the most sensitive and comprehensive assessment of the potential ecological impact of transgenic crops. Until these studies are completed, a moratorium on transgenic crops based on the precautionary principle should be imposed on the United States and other regions.

In the context of negotiations within the Convention on Biological Diversity (CBD) in 2000, 130 countries have shown the wisdom to adopt the precautionary principle by signing a global treaty that governs the trade of genetically modified organisms. United States (the US is not party to the BioSafety Protocol) export of GM food as aid to countries who have not yet implemented their own biosafety management regimes seems calculated to preempt and undermine the protocol. The precautionary principle holds that when a new technology may cause suspected harm, scientific uncertainty as to the scope and severity of the harm should not prevent precautionary action. Instead of requiring critics to prove that the technology poses potential damages, the producers of the technology shoulder the burden of presenting evidence that the technology is safe. The principle suggests that instead of using the criterion "absence of evidence" for serious environmental damage, the proper decision criterion should be the "evidence of absence," in other words, avoid "type II" statistical error: the error of assuming that no significant environmental risk is present when, in fact, risk exists. There is a clear need for independent testing and monitoring to make sure that self-generated data presented to government regulatory agencies is not biased or twisted to accommodate industry interests. Moreover, a worldwide moratorium should be enforced on GMOs until the questions raised both by credible scientists who are seriously investigating the ecological and health impacts of transgenic crops, and by the public at large, can be cleared up by independent bodies of scientists.

Many environmental and consumer groups advocating for a more sustainable agriculture demand continued support for ecologically based agricultural research. All the biological problems that biotechnology claims to address can be solved using agroecological approaches. The problem is that research at public institutions increasingly reflects the interests of private funding groups at the expense of the public good, and equivalent levels of research and development investment have not been made in alternative but effective approaches (Busch 1990). More research on biological controls, organic production systems, and general agroecological techniques is necessary. Civil society must request more research on alternatives to biotechnology by universities and other public organizations. There is also an urgent need to challenge the patent system and intellectual property rights intrinsic to the World Trade Organization (WTO), which not only provides multinational corporations with the right to seize and patent genetic resources, but also accelerates the rate at which market forces already encourage monoculture cropping with genetically uniform transgenic varieties. The Cartagena Protocol provides countries with an opportunity to assess the risks associated with GE crops before authorizing initial implementation. Zambia recently exercised its sovereign right and refused GE food aid, while Malawi, Mozambique, and Zimbabwe agreed to accept the shipments on condition that they were milled to prevent planting of the seed. If GE crops are planted, this could threaten exports of these countries to the European Union. Such countries are under considerable pressure and often suffer threats of WTO litigation.

CHAPTER FIVE

More Sustainable Alternatives to Biotechnology Do Exist

WHAT IS AGROECOLOGY?

Proponents of the second Green Revolution argue that developing countries should opt for an agro-industrial model that relies on standardized technologies and ever-increasing fertilizer and pesticide use to provide additional food supplies for growing populations and economies. In contrast, a growing number of farmers, nongovernmental organizations (NGOs), and sustainable agriculture advocates propose that instead of this capital- and input-intensive approach, developing countries should favor an agroecological model, which emphasizes biodiversity, recycling of nutrients, synergy among crops, animal, soils, and other biological components, as well as regeneration and conservation of resources (Altieri 1996).

A sustainable agricultural development strategy that is environmentally enhancing must be based on agroecological principles and on a more participatory approach for technology development and dissemination. Agroecology is the science that provides ecological principles for the design and management of sustainable and resource-conserving agricultural systems—offering several advantages for the development of farmer-friendly technologies. Agroecology relies on indigenous farming knowledge and selected low-input modern technologies to diversify production. The approach incorporates biological principles and local resources into the management of farming systems, and provides an environmentally sound and affordable way for small farmers to intensify production in marginal areas (Altieri et al. 1998).

It is estimated that approximately 1.9 to 2.2 billion people remain directly or indirectly untouched by modern agricultural technology. In Latin America, the rural population is projected to remain stable at 125 million until the year 2005, but over 61 percent of this population is poor, and this percentage is expected to increase. The projections for Africa are even more dramatic. The majority of the rural poor (about 370 million of the poorest) live in areas that are resource-poor, highly heterogeneous, and risk-prone. Their agricultural systems are small-scale, complex, and diverse. The worst poverty is often located in arid or semiarid zones, and in mountains and hills that are ecologically vulnerable. Such farms and their complex farming systems pose tough challenges to researchers.

To be of benefit to the rural poor, agricultural research and development should operate on the basis of a "bottom-up" approach, using and building on the resources already available: local people, their knowledge, and their indigenous natural resources. This must also seriously take into consideration the needs, aspirations, and circumstances of small farmers through participatory approaches. From the standpoint of poor farmers, innovations must

- Save inputs and reduce costs
- Reduce risk
- Promote restoration and stewardship of marginal/fragile lands
- Be congruent with peasant farming systems
- Improve nutrition, health, and environment.

Precisely because of the above requirements, agroecology offers several advantages over Green Revolution and biotech approaches. Agroecological technologies are

- Based on indigenous knowledge and rationale
- Economically viable, accessible, and based on local resources
- Environmentally sound, and socially and culturally sensitive

* Risk averse; adapted to farmer circumstances
* Enhancements of total farm productivity and stability.

Thousands of examples exist of rural producers, in partnerships with NGOs and other organizations, promoting resource-conserving yet highly productive farming systems while meeting the above criteria. Increases in production of 50 to 100 percent are fairly common with most alternative production methods. In some of these systems, yields for crops that the poor rely on most—rice, beans, maize, cassava, potatoes, barley—have been increased several-fold, relying on labor and local know-how more than on expensive purchased inputs, and capitalizing on processes of intensification and synergy. More important than just yields, it is possible to raise total production significantly through diversification of farming systems, using available resources as much as possible (Uphoff and Altieri 1999).

Many examples of the application of agroecology are at work throughout the developing world. An estimated 1.45 million poor rural households covering about 3.25 million hectares have adopted resource conserving technologies. Some examples include the following (Pretty 1995):

* *Brazil:* 200,000 farmers using green manures/cover crops doubled maize and wheat yields.
* *Guatemala-Honduras:* 45,000 farmers using the

legume mucuna as a cover for soil conservation systems tripled maize yields in hillsides.

* *Mexico:* 100,000 small organic coffee producers increased production by half.
* *Southeast Asia:* 100,000 small rice farmers involved in integrated pest management (IPM) farmers' schools substantially increased yields while eliminating pesticides.
* *Kenya:* 200,000 farmers using legume-based agroforestry and organic inputs doubled maize yields.

Perhaps the best example of alternatives to GE crops is from Africa, where scientists confirmed the dramatic positive effects of crop rotations, intercropping, and biological control on the regulation of pests usually targeted by biotechnologists. Scientists at the International Center for Insect Physiology and Ecology (ICIPE) in Kenya developed a habitat management system to control Lepidoptera stemborers, potential primary targets to be controlled via Bt crops. The push-pull system uses plants (Napier grass and Sudan grass) in the borders of maize fields that act as trap crops, attracting stemborer colonization away from maize (the push), and two plants intercropped with maize (molasses grass and silverleaf) to repel the stemborers (the pull) (Khan et al. 2000). Border grasses also enhance the parasitization of stemborers by the wasp *Cotesia semamiae* and are important fodder plants. The leguminous silverleaf (*Desmodium uncinatum*) suppresses the parasitic weed *Striga* by a factor of forty when compared with maize monocrop. *Desmodium*'s nitrogen-fixing ability increases soil fertility; and it is an excellent forage. As an added bonus, sale of *Desmodium* seed is proving to be a new income-generating opportunity for women in the project areas. The push-pull system has been tested on over 450 farms in two districts of Kenya and has now been released for uptake by the national extension systems in East Africa. Participating farmers in the breadbasket of Trans Nzoia are reporting a 15 to 20 percent increase in maize yield. In the semiarid Suba district, which is plagued by both stemborers and *Striga,* a substantial increase in milk yield has occurred in the last four years, with farmers now being able to support increased numbers of dairy cows on fodder they produce. When farmers plant maize together with the push-pull plants, a return of US $2.30 for every dollar invested is made, as compared to only US $1.40 obtained by planting maize as a monocrop (Khan et al. 2000).

SOME SUCCESS STORIES FROM LATIN AMERICA

Stabilizing the Hillsides of Central America

Perhaps the major agricultural challenge in Latin America has been to design hillside cropping systems that are productive and reduce erosion. World Neighbors took on this challenge in Honduras in the mid-1980s. The program introduced soil conservation practices such as drainage and contour ditches, grass barriers, and rock walls, and organic fertilization methods, such as the use of chicken manure and inter-cropping with legumes. Grain yields tripled, and in some cases quadrupled, from 0.4 tons per hectare to 1.2 to 1.4 tons. The yield increase has ensured that the 1,200 families participating in the program have ample grain supplies.

Several NGOs in Central America have promoted the use of legumes as green manure, an inexpensive source of organic fertilizer. Farmers in northern Honduras are using velvet beans with excellent results. Corn yields are more than double the national average, erosion and weeds are under control, and land preparation costs are lower. Taking advantage of well-established farmer-to-farmer networks in Nicaragua, more than 1,000 peasants recovered degraded land in the San Juan watershed in just one year after using this simple technology. These farmers have decreased use of chemical fertilizers from 1,900 to 400 kilograms per hectare, while increasing yields from 700 to 2,000 kilograms per hectare. Their production costs are about 22 percent lower than those for farmers using chemical fertilizers and monocultures. Moreover, hillside farmers adapting these soil conservation systems suffered significantly lower damage from mud slides and soil loss than monoculture farms during hurricane Mitch in 1998.

Recreating Inca Agriculture

In 1984, several NGOs and state agencies assisted local farmers in Puno, Peru to reconstruct ancient systems (*waru-warus*) consisting of raised fields surrounded by ditches filled with water. These fields produced bumper crops despite killing frosts common at altitudes of 13,123 feet. The combination of raised beds and canals moderates soil temperature, extending the growing season and leading to higher productivity on the waru-warus than on chemically fertilized normal pampa soils. In the district of Huatta, the waru-warus have produced annual potato yields of eight to fourteen metric tons per hectare, contrasting favorably with the average regional potato yields of one to four metric tons per hectare.

Various NGOs and governmental agencies in the Colca Valley of southern Peru have sponsored terrace reconstruction by offering peasants low-interest loans or seeds and other inputs to restore abandoned terraces. First-year yields of potatoes, maize, and barley showed a 43 to 65 percent increase compared to yields from sloping fields. A native legume was used as a rotational or associated crop on the terraces to fix nitrogen, minimizing fertilizer needs and increasing production. Studies in Bolivia, where native legumes have been used as rotational crops, show that though yields are greater in chemically fertilized and mechanically operated potato fields, energy costs are higher and net economic benefits lower than with the agroecological system.

Integrated Farms

A number of NGOs have promoted diversified farms in which each component of the farming system biologically reinforces the other components—wastes from one component, for instance, become inputs to another. Since 1980, the NGO Centers for Education and Training (CET) has helped peasants in south central Chile reach year-round food self-sufficiency while rebuilding the productive capacity of the land. Small model farm systems, consisting of polycultures and rotating sequences of forage and food crops, forest and fruit trees, and animals, have been set up. Components are chosen according to their nutritional contributions to subsequent rotations, their adaptability to local agro-climatic conditions, local peasant consumption patterns, and market opportunities.

Soil fertility of these farms has improved, and no serious pest or disease problems have appeared. Fruit trees and forage crops achieve higher than average yields, and milk and egg production far exceeds that of conventional high-input farms. A nutritional analysis shows that, for a typical family, the integrated system produces 250 percent surplus of protein, 80 and 550 percent surpluses of vitamin A and C, respectively, and 330 percent surplus of calcium. If all of the farm output were sold at wholesale prices, the family could generate a monthly net income one and a half times greater than the monthly legal minimum wage in Chile, while dedicating only a few hours per week to the farm. The time freed up is used by farmers for other on- and off-farm income-generating activities.

Recently, a Cuban NGO helped establish a number of integrated farming systems in cooperatives in the province of Havana. Several polycultures, such as cassava-beans-maize, cassava-tomato-maize, and sweet potato–maize were tested in the cooperatives. The productivity of these polycultures was 1.45 to 2.82 times greater than the productivity of the monocultures. The use of green manure ensured a production of squash equivalent to that obtainable by applying 175 kilograms of urea per hectare. In addition, green manure improved the physical and chemical characteristics of the soil and effectively broke the cycle of insect pest infestations.

The examples summarized above (see also Altieri 2000) are a small sample of the thousands of successful experiences of sustainable agriculture implemented at the local level. Data have shown that over time agroecological systems exhibit more stable levels of total production per unit area than high-input systems; produce economically favorable rates of return; provide a return to labor and other inputs sufficient for a livelihood acceptable to small farmers and their families; and ensure soil protection and conservation and enhance agro-biodiversity. More importantly, these experiences, which emphasize farmer-to-farmer research and grassroots extension approaches, represent countless demonstrations of talent, creativity, and scientific capability in rural communities. They point to the fact that human resource development is the cornerstone of any strategy aimed at increasing options for rural people and especially resource-poor farmers.

ORGANIC FARMING

Agroecological approaches can also benefit medium to large farms involved in commercial agriculture in the developing world, as well as the US and Europe (Lampkin 1990). Much of the area under organic farming is based on agroecology and is widespread throughout the world, reaching about 57 million acres of land under organic management, of which 26.2 million acres and 8 million acres are in Australia and Argentina respectively. Most is devoted to extensive grazing. More than 9 million acres are under certified organic farming in Europe and about 3 million in the United States. In Germany alone there are about 8,000 organic farms occupying about 2 percent of the total arable land. In Italy, organic farms number around 18,000, occupying about 3 million acres, and in Austria about 20,000 organic farms account for 10 percent of total agricultural output.

In Latin America organic farming accounts for 0.5 percent of the total agricultural land or about twelve million acres. In North America about 3.5 million acres are certified organic (45,000 organic farms), occupying 0.25 percent of the total agricultural land.

In the United States the organic acreage doubled between 1992 and 1997. In 1999 the retail organic produce industry generated US $6 billion in profit. In California organic foods are one of the fastest-growing segments of the agricultural economy, with retail sales growing at 2 to 25 percent per year for the past six years. Cuba is the only country undergoing a massive conversion to organic farming, promoted by the drop of fertilizer, pesticide, and petroleum imports after the collapse of trade relations with the Soviet bloc in 1990. By massively promoting agroecological techniques in both urban and rural areas, productivity levels in the island have recovered.

Research has shown that organic farms can be as productive as conventional ones, but without using agrochemicals. They also consume less energy and save soil and water. A strong body of evidence suggests that organic methods can produce enough food for all—and do it from one generation to the next without depleting natural resources or harming the environment. In 1989 the National Research Council wrote up case studies of eight organic farms that ranged from a 400-acre grain/livestock farm in Ohio to 1,400 acres of grapes in California and Arizona. The organic farms' average yields were generally equal to or better than the average yields of the conventional high-intensity farms surrounding them—once again showing they could be sustained year after year without costly synthetic inputs (National Research Council 1984).

In Washington State (USA), researchers reported that organic apple orchards that retained some level of plant diversity gave apple yields similar to conventional and integrated orchards. Data showed that the low-external input organic system ranked first in environmental and economic sustainability. This system exhibited higher profitability, greater energy efficiency, and lower negative environmental impact (Reaganold et al. 2001).

Recent research includes long-term studies such as the one conducted at the Farming Systems Trial at the Rodale Institute, a nonprofit research facility near Kutztown, Pennsylvania. Three kinds of experimental plots have been tested side by side for nearly two decades. One is a standard high-intensity rotation of corn and soybeans in which commercial fertilizers and pesticides have been used. Another is an organic system in which a rotation of grass/legume forage has been added and fed to cows, whose manure is then returned to the land. The third is an organic rotation in which soil fertility has been maintained solely with legume cover crops that have been plowed under. All three kinds of plots have been equally profitable in market terms. Corn yields have differed by less than 1 percent. The rotation with manure has far surpassed the other two in building soil organic matter and nitrogen, and it has leached fewer nutrients into groundwater. During the record drought of 1999, the chemically dependent plots yielded just sixteen bushels of soybeans per acre; the legume-fed organic fields delivered thirty bushels per acre, and the manure-fed organic fields delivered twenty-four bushels per acre.

In what must be the longest-running organic trial in the world—150 years—England's Rothamsted Experimental Station (also known as the Institute of Arable Crops Research) reports that its organic manured plots have delivered wheat yields of 1.58 tons per acre, compared to synthetically fertilized plots that have yielded 1.55 tons per acre. That may not seem like much, but the manured plots contain six times the organic matter found in the chemically treated plots.

The evidence shows that, in many ways, organic farming conserves natural resources and protects the environment more than conventional farming. Research also shows that soil erosion rates are lower in organic farms, and that levels of biodiversity are higher in organic farming systems than in conventional ones. The rationale behind each system is significantly different: organic farms are based on the assumption that at any given time some of the acreage is planted with legume green manure that will be plowed under or fodder crop that will go to feed cows, whose manure will be returned to the soil. The chemical farms are based on a profoundly different assumption: that their survival depends on a fertilizer factory somewhere that is consuming vast amounts of fossil fuels and emitting greenhouse gases.

WHAT IS NEEDED?

There is no question that small farmers located in marginal environments in the developing world can produce much of their needed food. The evidence is conclusive: New approaches and technologies spearheaded by farmers, local governments, and NGOs around the world are already making a sufficient contribution to food security at the household, national, and regional levels. A variety of agroecological and participatory approaches in many countries show very positive outcomes even under adverse conditions. Potentials include raising cereal yields from 50 to 200 percent, increasing stability of production through diversification and soil/water management, improving diets and income with appropriate support and spread of these approaches, and contributing to national food security and to exports (Uphoff and Altieri 1999). Importantly, the agroecological process requires participation and enhancement of the farmers' ecological literacy about their farms and resources, laying the foundation for empowerment and continuous innovation by rural communities.

Whether the potential and spread of these thousands of local agroecological innovations is realized depends on investments, policies, and attitude changes on the part of researchers and policy makers. Major changes must be made in institutions, research and development, and policies to make sure that agroecological alternatives are adopted, made equitably and broadly accessible, and multiplied so that their full benefit for sustainable food security can be realized. Existing subsidies and policy incentives for conventional chemical approaches must be dismantled. Corporate control over the food system must also be challenged. Governments and international public organizations must encourage and support effective partnerships between NGOs, local universities, and farmer organizations in order to assist and empower poor farmers to achieve food security, income generation, and natural resource conservation.

Equitable market opportunities must also be developed, emphasizing fair trade and other mechanisms that link farmers and consumers more directly. The ultimate challenge is to increase investment and research in agroecology and scale up projects that have already proven successful to thousands of other farmers. This will generate a meaningful impact on the income, food security, and environmental well being of the world's population, especially of the millions of poor farmers as yet untouched by—or already adversely impacted by—conventional modern agricultural technology.

Glossary

A

adaptation: Process by which an organism undergoes modification so that its functions are more suited to its environment and its changes.

adaptive mutation or directed mutation: Phenomenon whereby bacteria and yeast cells in stationary (nongrowing) phase have some way of producing or selectively retaining only the most appropriate mutations that enable them to make use of new substrates for growth.

agbiotech: Short for agricultural biotechnology; the organized application of genetic manipulations to plants.

Agrobacterium tumefaciens: Bacterium that causes crown gall disease in a range of dicotyledonous plants, especially coastal members of the genus Pinus. The bacterium can enter dead or broken plant cells in a living organism and transfer a tumor-inducing portion of DNA in the form of a plasmid. The plasmid then integrates into the plant's own genetic material, constituting a natural form of genetic engineering. Strains of *A. tumefaciens* can be artificially engineered to introduce selected foreign genes of choice into plant cells. By growing the infected cells in tissue culture, whole plants can be regenerated in which every cell carries the foreign gene.

allele: From *allelomorph*, meaning one of a series of possible, alternative forms of a given gene that differ in DNA sequence but produce a similar product; for instance a blood group or plant protein.

allergen: Substance that causes the body to react hypersensitively to it.

allotransplantation: Transplantation of cells, tissues, or organs from another member of the same species.

amino acid: Organic acid carrying an amino acid group (-NH2). There are twenty different amino acids, which are joined together in a defined order to make up linear molecules of proteins, each of which contains hundreds of amino acids.

antibiotic: Substance that acts to destroy or inhibit the growth of a microbe (e.g., bacteria or fungi).

antibody: Common name for an immunoglobulin protein molecule that reacts with a specific antigen.

antigen: Foreign substance capable of eliciting an immunological response in a vertebrate animal usually of a humoral variety and including production of an antibody specific to the antigen's structural makeup.

artificial selection: Choosing by humans of a genotype that contributes to the genetic types making up the succeeding generations for a given organism or plant.

B

Bacillus: Genus of rod-shaped bacteria. *Bacillus thuringiensis* is a spore-forming soil bacillus that grows in the soils of many regions and is the source of the toxoid used in genetic engineering (see Bt toxoid).

bacterium: Single cell microscopic organism in the Prokaryote kingdom.

baculovirus: Virus that normally infects insects.

bioengineering: Construction of a genetically controlled plant or animal by transferring genes from an otherwise genetically incompatible organism to create a novel function or product.

biological species: Groups of individuals that freely share a common set of genes and are reproductively isolated from other groups so that interbreeding usually cannot occur.

biopharming: The production of biopharmaceuticals in domestic animals.

biosecurity: Measures to protect from infection.

biotechnology: Combination of biochemistry, genetics, microbiology, and engineering to develop products and organisms of commercial value.

bottleneck effect: Fluctuation in gene frequencies brought about by the abrupt contraction of a large population into a smaller one, which then expands again with an altered gene pool.

Brassica: Genus of plants that includes broccoli and cabbage.

breeding: Controlled propagation of plants or animals.

bromoxynil: Bromine-containing herbicide produced by Rhône-Poulenc Company under the name Buctril.

Bt toxoid: Crystalline proteins derived from some strains of *Bacillus thuringiensis* that are activated to become poisonous in the alkaline environment of an insect larva's intestinal tract.

C

carcinogen: An agent, usually a chemical, which causes cancer.

cell: Smallest unit of all living things, capable of self-replication.

chromosome: Threadlike structure made up of DNA strands and proteins (histones and nonhistones) that carries genetic information in a linear sequence.

clone: Identical copy of an individual or gene, or the totality of all the identical copies made from an individual or a gene. In genetics, the clone is identical in genetic makeup to the original.

cloning: The propagation of genetically exact duplicates of an organism by a means other than sexual reproduction.

crop lineage: Descendants of a single progenitor of a given food crop.

crossbreeding: *See* **outbreeding.**

crossing: Fertilization of one plant with the pollen of the other. Such cross-pollination can be accomplished, for example, by humans, insects, or the wind, and can be intentional or not. When crossed by humans, however, some measure of intention is often assumed.

cultivar: Variety of plants produced through selective breeding by humans and maintained by cultivation.

D

Darwinian evolution: Preferential reproduction of genetically varied organisms with specific adaptations that permit their differential survival.

deoxyribonucleic acid (see DNA): Molecular basis for heredity.

diploid: Having a double genetic complement; the genetic material contributed from two haploid gametes.

DNA: Genetic material of cells comprised of two long chains of alternating phosphate and deoxyribose units, arrayed in an ascending/descending double helix and joined by hydrogen bonds.

DNA sequence: Linear array of complimentary bases adenine and thymine, or cystosine and guanine, which spells out the genetic code.

dominant: Form of expression in a gene; the phenotype of the dominant form is expressed over the recessive form.

dominant allele: Allele that is expressed when only one copy is present in an individual, that is, in a heterozygous condition.

dominant gene: Gene whose products are expressed when only one form of the gene is present as a single allele.

E

ecosystem: Composite of all the organisms of a given place interacting with the environment.

ecosystem disruption: Any perturbation to either the structure or function of an ecosystem.

epigenetic: Developmental. Any process not involving change in DNA base sequence in the genome.

epistasis: Interaction between genes.

essential amino acid: One of eight amino acids not synthesized in the human body. Includes phenylalanine, methionine, lysine, tryptophan, valine, leucine, isoleucine, and threonine.

estrogenic: Having the properties of an estrogen, e.g., in stimulating cell growth or proliferation in specific sexual target tissues.

eukaryotes: Superkingdom made up of organisms whose cells contain a true membrane-lined nucleus.

F

flavone: Aromatic molecule (containing a benzene ring as a core molecule) significant in the communication of legume plant to rhizobium and bradyrhizobium.

flavonoids: Molecules found in some plants that may have unpredictable biological properties, often antioxidant or hormonal in nature.

fitness: The ability to survive to reproductive age and produce viable offspring. Also refers to the frequency distribution of reproductive success for a population of sexually mature adults.

G

gene: Unit of heredity consisting of a sequence of DNA bases with "start" and "stop" information along with the base sequences for a specified protein.

gene amplification: Process where genes or sequences of DNA in the genome are greatly increased in number of copies.

gene bank: For plants, normally a temperature and humidity controlled facility used to store seed (or other reproductive materials) for future use in research and breeding programs. Also called seed banks.

gene cloning: Technique of making many copies of a gene, isolating the gene, and identifying it.

gene expression: In molecular genetics, usually means the eventual appearance of the polypeptide encoded by the gene.

gene silencing: Process (or processes) in which certain genes in the genome are prevented from being expressed, by chemical modifications and other means.

gene splicing: Creation of genetic combinations by intentionally interspersing a novel gene sequence into an existing genome, usually in bacteria.

genetic code: Code establishing the correspondence between the sequence of bases in nucleic acids (DNA and the complementary RNA) and the sequence of amino acids and proteins.

genetic diversity: In a group such as a population or species, the possession of a variety of genetic traits and alleles that frequently result in differing expression in different individuals.

genetic engineering: Experimental or industrial technologies used to alter the genome of a living cell so that it can produce more or different molecules than it is already programmed to make. The manipulation of genes to bypass normal or asexual reproduction.

genetic fingerprinting: Method probably initially developed by Alec Jeffreys which enables genetic relationships between close relatives to be established using DNA technologies.

genetic information: Data contained in a sequence of bases in a molecule of DNA.

genetic marker: Any segment of DNA that can be identified, or whose chromosomal location is known, so that it can be used as a reference point to map or locate other genes. Any gene that has an identifiable phenotype that can be used to track the presence or absence of other genes on the same piece of DNA transferred into a cell.

genetic resources: As used in this book, the term is essentially synonymous with germplasm, except that it carries with it a stronger implication that the material has or is seen as having economic or utilitarian value.

genome: All of the genes carried by a given organism.

genotype: The genetic identity of an individual.

germplasm: Material in the germ cells that supposedly accounts for the unchanging hereditary influence that is passed on to subsequent generations.

glyphosate: Active ingredient in the herbicide Roundup, marketed by Monsanto.

GMO: Abbreviation for genetically modified organism. A plant or animal containing permanently altered genetic material.

H

haploid: Containing only half the normal complement of chromosomes. The genetic complement of the gametes.

herbicide: Pesticide intended to affect plants. A chemical with killing or growth inhibiting effects on plants.

heterozygote: Individual zygote with two different alleles of a gene.

heterozygous: Condition in which two different alleles of the gene are present in an individual zygote.

homogeneity: Having the same form or content.

homologous: Similar, derived from a common ancestor. In diploid organisms, one member of a pair of matching chromosomes.

homozygosity: Having the same allele on both parental chromosomal strands. The state of being homozygous.

homozygote: Individual zygote with two identical alleles of the gene.

horizontal gene transfer: Transfer of genes from one individual to another, of the same or different species, usually by means other than cross-breeding.

hybrid: Organism derived from two distinct, and usually homozygous, parental lines.

I

inbred line: In plant breeding, a nearly homozygous line usually originating by continued self-fertilization, accompanied by selection. *See also* **pure line.**

inbreeding: Mating of individual organisms more closely related than organisms mating at random.

introgression: Introduction of genes from one member of the species into another where the donor is often geographically or morphologically distant from the recipient. *See* **introgressive hybridization.**

introgressive hybridization: Incorporation of genes of one species into the gene pool of another, usually resulting in a population of individuals that continue to represent the more common parental line, but also possess some of the characteristics of the donor parent lineage.

isoflavone: Aromatic signal substance involved in the nodulation of legumes.

isogenic: Having the same genetic makeup.

L

landrace: Population of plants, typically genetically heterogeneous, commonly developed in traditional agriculture from many years—even centuries—of farmer-directed selection, and specifically adapted to local conditions.

legume: Plant family characterized by a pea-like flower morphology. Many but not all legumes are nodulated and form nitrogen-fixing symbioses with soil bacteria called rhizobium, bradyrhizobium, and azorhizobium.

Lepidoptera: Genus that includes the moths and butterflies. Larvae of the same.

M

messenger RNA: RNA intermediate in protein synthesis containing a transcribed copy of the gene sequence specifying the amino acid sequence of the polypeptide it encodes.

mobile genetic element: Sequence of DNA that can transpose (or move) from one place to another in the genome of a cell. Also called transposon or transposable genetic element.

molecule: Assembly of atoms into a structure maintained by interatomic bonds (e.g., hydrogen or carbon-carbon bonds).

monoculture: Growth or colony containing a single, pure genetic line of organisms. Genetically uniform line of plants or organisms derived from tissue culture.

mutation: Sudden heritable variation in a gene or chromosomal structure.

N

neomycin transferase: A bacterial gene encoding resistance to several antibiotics (Kanamycin, neomycin) widely used as a selectable marker.

nitrogen fixation: Process by which atomic nitrogen is made accessible to plants by conversion to metabolize chemicals like ammonia.

nodule: Outgrowth from the roots (or stems in some cases) of legumes induced by bacteria or exogenous agents such as bacterial derived nodulation factors or auxin transport inhibitors.

O

outbreeding: Making crosses between distantly related members of the same species (syn. outcrossing).

P

pathogen: Any agent that can cause disease.

phenotype: Expressed characteristics or an expressed character of an organism due to its genotype.

plant growth regulator: Broad class of chemicals that control the growth of plants. Many are also natural compounds found within plants, where they may act as hormones.

plasmid: Circular, covalently closed DNA molecule commonly found in bacteria. Often used as a cloning vector in genetic engineering.

pleiotropy: A phenomenon whereby a single gene affects multiple traits.

pollination: Process by which the male sex cells of a plant's anther fertilize the stigma.

polygenes: Many genes (hypothetically) affecting a character, each having a small, additive effect on the character.

prokaryotes: Superkingdom containing forms of life without cell walls. Microorganisms lacking a membrane-bound nucleus containing chromosomes.

promoter: Regulatory region of a gene involved in the control of RNA polymerase binding to the target gene.

propagation: Asexual reproduction and growth of plants from tissue culture, cuttings, or scions from a parent plant.

pure line: Genetically uniform (homozygous) population.

Q

QTL (qualitative trait locus): Term given to a genomic region which controls a phenotype by interaction with other genes (i.e., oil content in soybeans).

R

recombinant DNA techniques: Procedures used to join together DNA segments in a cell-free system (an environment outside of a celled organism).

recombination: Formation of new combinations of alleles or new genes that occurs when two pieces of DNA join or exchange parts.

reductionism: Doctrine that a complex system can be completely understood in terms of its simplest parts; for example, that an organism can be completely understood in terms of its genes, or a society in terms of its individuals.

reverse transcription: Reverse of transcription—making a copy of complementary DNA (cDNA) from an RNA sequence—catalyzed by the enzyme reverse transcriptase.

rhizobium: Bacteria able to form nodules with some legumes such as peas, alfalfa, and clover.

ribonuclease: Enzyme that breaks down RNA.

ribosomal RNA: RNA molecules that make up the ribosome.

ribosome: Organelle in the cell required for protein synthesis.

RNA (ribonucleic acid): Similar to DNA except for the sugar in the nucleotide unit, which is ribose instead of deoxyribose, and the base, which is uracil instead of thymine. RNA is the genetic material for RNA viruses.

Roundup Ready: Monsanto's brand name for plants (soybean) genetically engineered to be resistant to the herbicidal effects of glyphosate (Roundup).

S

seed bank: Collection of seed and germplasm from a broad cross section of plants or food crops, stored under liquid nitrogen for protracted periods.

selectable marker: A gene encoding resistance to an antibiotic added to a vector construct to allow easy selection of cells that contain the construct from the large majority of cells that do not.

shuttle vector: Artificially constructed vector that can replicate and transfer genes between two often distant species.

silencing: Shutdown of transcription of a gene, usually by methylation of C residues.

somatic cells: Cells of body tissues other than the germline.

soybean: *Glycine max (L) Marr,* a tropical legume of wide agronomic application. Nodulates with *Bradyrhizobium japonicum* and *Rhizobium fredii.*

species: Freely interbreeding group of organisms that is genetically isolated from closely related stocks from which it might otherwise share genes. In classification, the individuals within an order that freely interbreed (cf. genus and species: ex. *Glycine max*).

StarLink™: A brand of transgenic maize approved for animal feed only, but which also has been found in the human food supply.

T

T DNA: DNA encoded on a plasmid of Agrobacterium that integrates into the genome of a plant cell after being introduced into the cell by fusion.

teratogenic: Capable of producing birth defects or other reproductive harm, manifesting in a visible disorder in form or size.

transcription: Process of making a complementary sequence of the gene sequence in the genome, either used directly, as in the case of ribosomal RNAs (rRNAs) and transfer RNAs (tRNAs), or further processed into the messenger RNA, and translated into protein. The process is catalyzed by the enzyme known as DNA-dependent RNA polymerase.

transduction: Transfer of genes by viruses from one organism to another.

transfer RNA: RNA molecules that transfer specific amino acids to the messenger RNA so that the polypeptide it encodes can be synthesized.

transformation: Uptake of genes by one organism of DNA belonging to another organism of the same or different species.

transgene: A gene construct introduced into an organism by human intervention.

transgenesis: Science of interspecific movement of individual genes.

transgenic: Adjective describing an organism that contains genes not native to its genetic makeup.

transgenic organism: Organism created by genetic engineering, in which one or more foreign genes have been incorporated in its genome.

V

variety: Morphologically distinct subtypes of a given species and genus, e.g., a novel variety of corn.

vector: Carrier for transferring disease or genes, e.g., the mosquito is a vector for malaria. Viruses, plasmids, and transposons are vectors for genes. Aphids are vectors for transferring disease-causing viruses form one plant to another.

virus: Parasitic genetic element enclosed in a protein coat that can replicate in cells and form infectious particles, or remain dormant in the cell. Its genetic material can become integrated to the cell's genome to form provirus.

X

xenotransplantation: Transplantation of cells, tissues or organs from one species to another.

Z

zygote: A fertilized oocyte.

Resources

RELATED WEB SITES

Activist Network Squall
www.squall.co.uk/ind2.html

Agbio World Foundation
www.agbioforum.com

Australian Gene Ethics Network
www.geneethics.org

Ben & Jerry's
www.benjerry.com

Biosafety Bibliographical Database
www.icgeb.trieste.it/biosafety/bsfrel.htm

Biosafety Information Network and Advisory Service
(BINAS) (service of the United Nations Industrial
Development Organization)
www.binas.unido.org/binas/

Biotechnology Industry Organization
www.bio.org/welcome.html

British Natural Law Party Manifesto on GE
www.natural-law-party.org.uk

Calgene
www.calgene.com

California Food Policy Advocates
www.cfpa.net

Californians for Pesticide Reform (CPR)
www.pesticidereform.org

Campaign for Food Safety
www.purefood.org

Campaign to Label GE Food
www.thecampaign.org

Center for Ethics and Toxics
www.cetos.org

Certified Organic Food
www.gks.com

Consumers International
www.consumersinternational.org

Consumers Choice Council
www.consumerscouncil.org

Cooperative Resource from United Nations Industrial
Development Organization (Unido) and Organization
for Economic Cooperation and Development (OECD)
www.oecd.org/ehs/biobin

Corporate Watch
www.corpwatch.org

Council for Responsible Genetics
www.gene-watch.org

Farm Aid
www.farmaid.org

Food Research and Action Center
www.frac.org

Foundation on Economic Trends
www.foet.org

Free Range Activism Website
www.fraw.org.uk

ETC Group
www.etcgroup.org

Exposé of the rBGH Scandal
www.notmilk.com

Food First/Institute for Food and Development Policy
www.foodfirst.org

Fox BGH Story
www.foxBGHsuit.com

Friends of the Earth Anti-GE Campaign
www.foe.co.uk/camps/foodbio/genetic.html

Frost & Sullivan, Pro-Biotech Marketing
www.frost.com

Genetic Engineering and Its Dangers, Dr. Ron Epstein,
San Francisco State University
http://online.sfsu.edu/%7Erone/GEessays/gedanger.htm

Genetic Engineering Network
www.dmac.co.uk/gen.html

Genetic ID
www.genetic-id.com

Genetically Manipulated Food News, GE Archive
http://home.intekom.com/tm_info

Genetic Resources Action International (GRAIN)
www.grain.org

Greenpeace International
www.greenpeace.org/international_en

Greenpeace USA
www.greenpeaceusa.org

Henry A. Wallace Institute for Alternative Agriculture
www.ibiblio.org/InterGarden/permaculture/mailarchives
/permaculture-links/msg00195.html

Humane Farming Association
www.hfa.org

Institute for Agriculture and Trade Policy
www.iatp.org

Institute of Development Studies (IDS)
www.ids.ac.uk/biotech

International Center for Technology Assessment
www.icta.org

International Service for the Acquisition of Agri-Biotech
Applications (ISAAA)
www.isaaa.org

Monsanto
www.monsanto.com

Monsanto's Information on Roundup Ready Crops
www.monsanto.com/monsanto/layout/products/
productivity/roundup/default.asp /

Mothers for Natural Law
www.safe-food.org

National Campaign for Sustainable Agriculture
www.sustainableagriculture.net

National Farmers Union
www.nfu.org

National Organic Program
www.ams.usda.gov/nop/

Natural Law Party (United States)
www.natural-law.org/index.html

Novartis
www.novartis.com

Organic Trade Association
www.ota.com

Panos Institute
www.panosinst.org

Pesticide Action Network North America (PANNA)
www.panna.org

Physicians and Scientists for Responsible Application of
Science and Technology
www.psrast.org

Public Citizen
www.citizen.org

Pure Food Campaign
www.purefood.org

Rachel's Environment and Health Weekly
www.rachel.org

Summaries of Biotechnology, Genetic Engineering
www.ucsusa.org/agriculture/biotech.html

Sustainable Agriculture Network
www.sare.org/san/

Third World Network
www.twnside.org.sg

UK List of GE-free Foods
www.safe-food.org

UK Soil Association
www.soilassociation.org

Union of Concerned Scientists
www.ucsusa.org

Vegetarian Society UK
www.vegsoc.org

Washington Biotechnology Action Council (WashBAC)
http://washbac.org/

Whole Foods Market
www.wholefoods.com

WWW Virtual Library on Biotechnology
www.cato.com/biotech/

Bibliography

Alstad, D. N., and D. A. Andow. 1995. Managing the evolution of insect resistance to transgenic plants. *Science* 268:1894–1896.

Altieri, M. A. 1994. *Biodiversity and Pest Management in Agroecosystems*. New York: Haworth Press.

———. 1995. *Agroecology: The Science of Sustainable Agriculture*. Boulder, CO: Westview Press.

———. 2000a. The ecological impacts of transgenic crops on agroecosystem health. *Ecosystem Health* 6:13–23.

———. 2000b. Developing sustainable agricultural systems for small farmers in Latin America. *Natural Resources Forum* 24:97–105.

———. 2003. The sociocultural and food security impacts of genetic pollution via transgenic crops of traditional varieties in Latin American centers of peasant agriculture. *Bulletin of Science, Technology, and Society* 23:1-10.

Altieri, M. A., P. Rosset, and L. A. Thrupp. 1998. The potential of agroecology to combat hunger in the developing world (*International Food Policy and Research Institute 2020 Brief No. 55*). Washington, DC: International Food Policy Research Institute.

Andow, D. A. 1991. Vegetation diversity and arthropod

population response. *Annual Review of Entomology* 36:561–586.

Aristide, J. B. 2000. *Eyes of the Heart: Seeking a Path for the Poor in the Age of Globalization*. Monroe, ME: Common Courage Press.

Boucher, D. H., ed. 1999. *The Paradox of Plenty: Hunger in a Bountiful World*. Oakland, CA: Food First Books.

Brummer, E. C. 1998. Diversity, stability and sustainable American agriculture. *Agronomy Journal* 90:1–2.

Burks, A. W., and R. L. Fuchs. 1995. Assessment of the endogenous allergens in glyphosate-tolerant and commercial soybean varieties. *Journal of Allergy and Clinical Immunology* 96:6–13.

Busch, L., W. B. Lacy, J. Burkhardt, and L. Lacy. 1990. *Plants, Power and Profit*. Oxford, UK: Basil Blackwell.

Carpenter, J. E., and L. P. Gianessi. 1999. Herbicide tolerant soybeans: why growers are adopting Roundup Ready varieties. *Agbioforum* 2:2–9.

Casper, R., and J. Landsmann. 1992. The biosafety results of field tests of genetically modified plants and microorganisms. *Proceeding of the Second International Symposium Goslar*. P. K. Launders, ed., 89–97. Braunschweig, Germany: Biologische Bundesanstalt.

Chilcutt, C. F. and B. E. Tabashnik. 2004. Contamination of refuges by *Bacillus thuringiensis* toxin genes from transgenic maize. *PANS* 101:7256–7254.

Conroy, M. T., D. L. Murray, and P. Rosset. 1996. *A Cautionary Fable: Failed US Development Policy in Central America*. Boulder, CO: Lynne Rienner Publishers.

Conway, G. R. 1997. *The Doubly Green Revolution: Food*

for All in the 21st Century. London, UK: Penguin Books.

Conway, G. R., and J. N. Pretty. 1991. *Unwelcome Harvest: Agriculture and Pollution*. London, UK: Earthscan.

Crucible Group. 1994. *People, Plants and Patents*. Ottawa, Canada: International Development Research Center.

Darmancy, H. 1994. The impact of hybrids between genetically modified crop plants and their related species: introgression and weediness. *Molecular Ecology* 3:37–40.

Donnegan, K. K., C. J. Palm, V. J. Fieland, L. A. Porteus, L. M. Ganis, D. L. Scheller, and R. J. Seidler. 1995. Changes in levels, species, and DNA fingerprints of soil microorganisms associated with cotton expressing the *Bacillus thuringiensis* var. Kurstaki endotoxin. *Applied Soil Ecology* 2:111–124.

Donnegan, K. K., and R. Seidler. 1999. Effects of transgenic plants on soil and plant microorganisms. *Recent Research Developments in Microbiology* 3:415–424.

Duffy, M. 1999. Does planting GMO seed boost farmers' profits? *Leopold Center for Sustainable Agriculture Letter* 11(3):1–5.

Duke, S. O. 1996. *Herbicide Resistant Crops: Agricultural, Environmental, Economic, Regulatory, and Technical Aspects*. Boca Raton, FL: Lewis Publishers.

Firbank, L. G. 2003. Introduction to the farm scale evaluations of genetically modified herbicide-tolerant crops. *Philosophical Translations of the Royal Society London* 358:1777–1778.

Fowler, C., and Mooney, P. 1990. *Shattering: Food, Politics, and the Loss of Genetic Diversity*. Tucson: University of Arizona Press.

Ghaffaradeh, M. F., G. Prechac, and R. M. Cruse. 1999. Grain yield response of corn, soybean and oat grain in a strip intercropping system. *American Journal of Alternative Agriculture* 4:171–175.

Gill, D. S. 1995. Development of herbicide resistance in annual ryegrass populations in the cropping belt of western Australia. *Australian Journal of Experimental Agriculture* 3:67–72.

Goldberg, R. J. 1992. Environmental concerns with the development of herbicide-tolerant plants. *Weed Technology* 6:647–652.

Gould, F. 1994. Potential and problems with high-dose strategies for pesticidal engineered crops. *Biocontrol Science and Technology* 4:451–461.

Green, M. B., A. M. LeBaron, and W. K. Moberg, eds. 1990. *Managing Resistance to Agrochemicals*. Washington, DC: American Chemical Society.

Greenland, D. J. 1997. *The Sustainability of Rice Farming*. Wallingford, England: CAB International.

Gresshoff, P. M. 1996. *Technology Transfer of Plant Biotechnology*. Boca Raton, FL: CRC Press.

Hansen, M. K. 1999. *Genetic Engineering Is Not an Extension of Conventional Plant Breeding*. New York: Consumer Policy Institute.

Hilbeck, A., A. M. Baumgartnet, P. M. Fried, and F. Bigler. 1998. Effects of transgenic *Bacillus thuringiensis* corn fed prey on mortality and development time of immature *Crysoperla carnea* (Neuroptera: Chrysopidae). *Environmental Entomology* 27:460–487.

Hilbeck, A., W. J. Moar, M. Putzai-carey, A. Filippini, and F. Bigler. 1999. Prey-mediated effects of Cry1Ab toxin and protoxin on the predator *Chrysoperla carnea*. *Entomology, Experimental and Applied* 91:305–316.

Hindmarsh, R. 1991. The flawed 'sustainable' promise of genetic engineering. *The Ecologist* 21:196–205.

Hobbelink, H. 1991. *Biotechnology and the Future of World Agriculture*. London: Zed Books.

Holt, J. S., S. Powles, and J. A. M. Holtum. 1993. Mechanisms and agronomic aspects of herbicide resistance. *Annual Review of Plant Physiology and Plant Molecular Biology* 44:203–229.

Holt, J. S., and H. M. Le Baron. 1990. Significance and distribution of herbicide resistance. *Weed Technology* 4:141–149.

Hruska, A. J., and M. Lara Pavon. 1997. *Transgenic Plants in Mesoamerican Agriculture*. Honduras: Zamorano.

James, C. 1997. Global status of transgenic crops in 1997. *International Service for the Acquisition of Agri-Biotech Applications,* 30. Ithaca, NY: ISAAA Briefs. Available on the World Wide Web: *www.isaaa.org/frbriefs.htm.*

Jordan, C. F. 2001 Genetic engineering, the farm crisis and world hunger. *BioScience* 52:523–529.

Kendall, H. W., R. Beachy, T. Eismer, F. Gould, R. Herdt, P. H. Ravon, J. Schell, and M. S. Swaminathan. 1997. Biotechnology of crops. *Report of the World Bank Panel on Transgenic Crops,* 1–30. Washington DC: World Bank.

Kennedy, G. G., and M. E. Whalon. 1995. Managing pest resistance to *Bacillus thuringiensis* endotoxins: constraints and incentives to implementations. *Journal of Economic Entomology* 88:454–460.

Khan, Z. R., J. A. Pickett, J. van der Berg, and C. M. Woodcock. 2000. Exploiting chemical ecology and species diversity: stemborer and Striga control for maize in Africa. *Pest Management Science* 56:1–6.

Kleinman, D. L., and J. Kloppenburg. 1988. Biotechnology and university-industry relations: policy issues in research and the ownership of intellectual property at a land grant university. *Policy Studies Journal* 17:83–96.

Kloppenburg, J. 1998. *First the Seed: The Political Economy of Plant Technology*. Cambridge: Cambridge University Press.

Krimsky, S., and R. P. Wrubel. 1996. *Agricultural Biotechnology and the Environment: Science, Policy and Social Issues*. Urbana, IL: University of Illinois Press.

Lampkin, N. 1990. *Organic Farming*. Ipswich, NY: Farming Press.

Lappé, F. M., and B. Bailey. 1998. *Against the Grain: Biotechnology and the Corporate Takeover of Food*. Monroe, ME: Common Courage Press.

Lappé, F. M., J. Collins, P. Rosset, and L. Esparza. 1998. *World Hunger: Twelve Myths,* second edition. New York: Grove Press.

Lappé, M. A., E. B. Bailey, C. H. Childers, and K. D. R. Setchell. 1999. Alterations in clinically important phytoestrogens in genetically modified, herbicide-tolerant soybeans. *Journal of Medicinal Food* 1:241–245.

Liu, Y. B., B. E. Tabasnik, T. J. Dennehy, A. L. Patin, A. C. Bartlett. 1999. Development time and resistance to Bt crops. *Nature* 400:519.

Losey, J. J. E., L. S. Rayor, and M.E. Carter. 1999. Transgenic pollen harms monarch larvae. *Nature* 399:214.

Lurquin, P. F. 2002. *High Tech Harvest: Understanding Genetically Modified Food Plants*. Boulder, CO: Westview Press.

Lutman, P. J. W., ed. 1999. Gene flow and agriculture:

relevance for transgenic crops. *British Crop Protection Council Symposium Proceedings* No. 72, 43–64. Staffordshire, England: British Crop Protection Council.

Mallet, J., and P. Porter. 1992. Preventing insect adaptations to insect resistant crops: are seed mixtures or refuge the best strategy? *Proceeding of the Royal Society of London Series B Biology Science* 250:165–169.

Mellon, M., and J. Rissler. 1999. *Now or Never: Serious New Plans to Save a Natural Pest Control.* Washington, DC: Union of Concerned Scientists.

Mellon, M. and J. Rissler. 2004. *Gone to Seed: Transgenic Contamination in the Conventional Seed Supply.* Cambridge: Union of Concerned Scientists.

Molnar, J. J., and H. Kinnucan. 1989. *Biotechnology and the New Agricultural Revolution.* Boulder, CO: Westview Press.

Murray, D. R. 2003. *Seeds of Concern: the Genetic Manipulation of Plants.* London: CABI Publishing.

National Research Council. 1984. *Alternative Agriculture.* Washington, DC: National Academy Press.
———. 1996. *Ecologically Based Pest Management.* Washington, DC: National Academy of Sciences.

Nicholls, C. I., and M. A. Altieri. 1997. Conventional agricultural development models and the persistence of the pesticide treadmill in Latin America. *International Journal of Sustainable Development and World Ecology* 4:93–111.

Obrycki, J. J., J. E. Losey, O. R. Taylor, and L. C. H. Jesse. 2001. Transgenic insecticidal corn: beyond insecticide toxicity to ecological complexity. *BioScience* 51: 353–361.

Office of Technology Assessment. 1992. *A New Techno-
    logical Era for American Agriculture*. Washington, DC:
    US Government Printing Office.
Onstad, D. W., and F. Gould. 1998. Do dynamics of crop
    maturation and herbivorous insect life cycle influence
    the risk of adaptation to toxins in transgenic host
    plants? *Environmental Entomology* 27:517–522.

Palm, C. J., D. L. Scheller, K. K. Donegan, and R. J. Seidler.
    1996. Persistence in soil of transgenic plant produced
    Bacillus thuringiensis var. Kustaki endotoxin. *Canadian
    Journal of Microbiology* 42:1258–1262.
Paoletti, M. G., and D. Pimentel. 1996. Genetic engineering
    in agriculture and the environment: assessing risks and
    benefits. *BioScience* 46:665–671.
Persley, G. J., and M. M. Lantin. 2000. *Agricultural
    Biotechnology and the Poor*. Washington DC:
    Consultative Group on International Agricultural
    Research.
Prakash, C. S., and G. Conko. 2004. Technology for life:
    how biotech will save millions from starvation. *The
    American Enterprise* 15:16–20.
Pretty, J. 1995. *Regenerating Agriculture: Policies and
    Practices for Sustainability and Self-reliance*. London:
    Earthscan.

Quist, D., and I. Chapela. 2001. Transgenic DNA intro-
    gressed into traditional maize landraces in Oaxaca,
    Mexico. *Nature* 414:541–543.

Radosevich, S. R., J. S. Holt, and C. M. Ghersa. 1996.
    Weed Ecology: Implications for Weed Management, sec-
    ond edition. New York: John Wiley and Sons.
Reaganold, J. P., J. D. Glover, P. K. Andrews, and H. R.

Hinnan. 2001. Sustainability of three apple production systems. *Nature* 410:926–930.

Rissler, J., and M. Mellon. 1996. *The Ecological Risks of Engineered Crops.* Cambridge, MA: MIT Press.

Robinson, R. A. 1996. *Return to Resistance: Breeding Crops to Reduce Pesticide Resistance.* Davis, CA: AgAccess.

Rosset, P. 1999. The multiple functions and benefits of small farm agriculture in the context of global trade negotiations, *Food First Policy Brief No. 4.* Oakland, CA: Institute for Food and Development Policy.

Royal Society. 1998. Genetically modified plants for food use. Statement 2/98. London: Royal Society.

Saxena, D., S. Flores, and G. Stotzky. 1999. Insecticidal toxin in root exudates from Bt corn. *Nature* 40:480.

Schuler, T. H., R. P. J. Potting, I. Dunholm, and G. M. Poppy. 1999. Parasitic behavior and Bt plants. *Nature* 400:825.

Snow, A. A., and P. Moran. 1997. Commercialization of transgenic plants: potential ecological risks. *BioScience* 47:86–96.

Steinbrecher, R. A. 1996. From green to gene revolution: the environmental risks of genetically engineered crops. *The Ecologist* 26:273–282.

Tabashnik, B. E. 1994a. Genetics of resistance to *Bacillus thuringiensis*. *Annual Review of Entomology* 39:47–49.
———. 1994b. Delaying insect adaptation to transgenic plants: seed mixtures and refugia reconsidered. *Proceedings of the Royal Society, London* 255:7–12.

Thrupp, L. A. 1998. *Cultivating Biodiversity: Agrobiodiversity for Food Security.* Washington DC: World Resources Institute.

Ticciati, L., and R. Ticciati. 1998. *Genetically Engineered Foods: Are They Safe?* New Canaan, CT: Keats Publishing.

Traynor, P. L., and J. H. Westwood. 1999. *Ecological Effects of Pest Resistance Genes in Managed Ecosystems.* Blacksburg, VA: Information Systems for Biotechnology.

Tripp, R. 1996. Biodiversity and modern crop varieties: sharpening the debate. *Agriculture and Human Values* 13:48–62.

United States Department of Agriculture. 1999. *Genetically Engineered Crops for Pest Management.* Washington DC: USDA Economic Research Service.

Uphoff, N., and M. A. Altieri. 1999. Alternatives to conventional modern agriculture for meeting world food needs in the next century (Report of a Bellagio Conference). Ithaca, NY: Cornell International Institute for Food, Agriculture, and Development.

Webber, D. J., ed. 1990. *Biotechnology, Assessing Social Impacts and Policy Implications.* Westport, CT: Greenwood Press.

About the Author

Miguel A. Altieri has been a faculty member at the University of California, Berkeley since 1980, where he is currently Professor of Entomology with the department of Environmental Science Policy and Management. During his tenure he has actively taught agroecology and sustainable agriculture at Berkeley as well as in a number of universities in Latin America and Europe. He is the author of ten books (among them the pioneering textbook *Agroecology: The Science of Sustainable Agriculture*) and of more than 200 scientific articles.

Dr. Altieri's research has focused on ways of enhancing biodiversity in agroecosystems to optimize biological pest control and the general ecological performance of agricultural systems. In the last few years he has been involved in implementing agroecology courses through long distance training in Mexico and South America, experience he now is extending to Europe and the US.

About Food First

Food First, also known as the Institute for Food and Development Policy, is a nonprofit research and education-for-action center dedicated to investigating and exposing the root causes of hunger in a world of plenty. It was founded in 1975 by Frances Moore Lappé, author of the bestseller *Diet for a Small Planet*, and food policy analyst Dr. Joseph Collins. Food First research has revealed that hunger is created by concentrated economic and political power, not by scarcity. Resources and decision-making are in the hands of a wealthy few, depriving the majority of land and jobs, and therefore of food.

Hailed by the *New York Times* as "one of the most established food think tanks in the country," Food First has grown to profoundly shape the debate about hunger and development.

But Food First is more than a think tank. Through books, reports, videos, media appearances, and speaking engagements, Food First experts not only reveal the often hidden roots of hunger, they show how individuals can get involved in bringing an end to the problem. Food First inspires action by bringing to light the courageous efforts of people around the world who are creating farming and food systems that truly meet people's needs.

How to Become a Member or Intern of Food First

BECOME A MEMBER OF FOOD FIRST

Private contributions and membership gifts form the financial base of Food First/Institute for Food and Development Policy. The success of the Institute's programs depends not only on its dedicated volunteers and staff, but on financial activists as well. Each member strengthens Food First's efforts to change a hungry world. We invite you to join Food First. As a member you will receive a twenty percent discount on all Food First books. You will also receive our quarterly publication, *Food First News and Views,* and timely *Backgrounders* that provide information and suggestions for action on current food and hunger crises in the United States and around the world. If you want to subscribe to our Internet newsletters, *Food Rights Watch and We Are Fighting Back,* send us an email at **foodfirst@foodfirst.org**. All contributions are tax-deductible.

BECOME AN INTERN FOR FOOD FIRST

There are opportunities for interns in research, advocacy, campaigning, publishing, computers, media, and publicity at Food First. Our interns come from around the world. They are a vital part of our organization and make our work possible.

To become a member or apply to become an intern, just call, visit our web site, or clip and return the attached coupon to

FOOD FIRST
398 60th Street, Oakland, CA 94618, USA
PHONE 510.654.4400
FAX 510.654.4551
EMAIL foodfirst@foodfirst.org
WEB www.foodfirst.org

You are also invited to give a gift membership to others interested in the fight to end hunger.

More Books from Food First

To Inherit the Earth: *The Landless Movement and the Struggle for a New Brazil*
ANGUS WRIGHT and WENDY WOLFORD
To Inherit the Earth tells the dramatic story of Brazil's Landless Workers' Movement, or MST, wherein many thousands of desperately poor, landless, jobless men and women have through their own nonviolent efforts secured rights to more than 20 million acres of unused farmland.
PAPERBACK, $15.95

Breakfast of Biodiversity: *The Truth about Rain Forest Destruction*
JOHN VANDERMEER and IVETTE PERFECTO
Why biodiversity is in such jeopardy around the world and what steps must be taken to slow the ravaging of rain forests.
PAPERBACK, $16.95

Earthsummit.biz: *The Corporate Takeover of Sustainable Development*
KENNY BRUNO and JOSHUA KARLINER
The story of the corporate cooptation of the rhetoric of social and environmental responsibility, with 18 muckraking case studies of the ways corporate behavior contradicts corporate PR.
PAPERBACK, $12.95

Sustainable Agriculture and Development: *Transforming Food Production in Cuba*
FERNANDO FUNES, LUIS GARCÍA, MARTIN BOURQUE,
NILDA PÉREZ, and PETER ROSSET
Unable to import food or farm chemicals and machines in the wake of the Soviet bloc's collapse and a tightening U.S. embargo, Cuba turned toward sustainable agriculture, organic farming, urban gardens, and

other techniques to secure its food supply. This book gives details of that remarkable achievement.

PAPERBACK, $18.95

The Future in the Balance: Essays on Globalization and Resistance
WALDEN BELLO
Edited with a preface by ANURADHA MITTAL
A new collection of essays by Third World activist and scholar Walden Bello on the myths of development as prescribed by the World Trade Organization and other institutions, and the possibility of another world based on fairness and justice.

PAPERBACK, $13.95

Views from the South: The Effects of Globalization and the WTO on Third World Countries
Foreword by JERRY MANDER
Afterword by ANURADHA MITTAL
Edited by SARAH ANDERSON
This rare collection of essays by Third World activists and scholars describes in pointed detail the effects of the WTO and other Bretton Woods institutions.

PAPERBACK, $12.95

Basta! Land and the Zapatista Rebellion in Chiapas
Revised edition
GEORGE A. COLLIER with ELIZABETH LOWERY QUARATIELLO
Foreword by PETER ROSSET
The classic on the Zapatistas in a new revised edition, including a preface by Roldolfo Stavenhagen, a new epilogue about the present challenges to the indigenous movement in Chiapas, and an updated bibliography.

PAPERBACK, $14.95

America Needs Human Rights
Edited by ANURADHA MITTAL and PETER ROSSET
This new anthology includes writings on understanding human rights, poverty in America, and welfare reform and human rights.

PAPERBACK, $13.95

The Paradox of Plenty: *Hunger in a Bountiful World*
Excerpts from Food First's best writings on world hunger and what we can do to change it.
PAPERBACK, $18.95

W E ENCOURAGE YOU to buy Food First Books from your local independent bookseller: if they don't have them in stock, they can usually order them for you fast. To find an independent bookseller in your area, go to **www.booksense.com**.

Food First books are also available through the major online booksellers (Powell's, Amazon, and Barnes and Noble), and through the Food First website, **www.foodfirst.org**. You can also order direct from our distributor, CDS, at 800.343.4499. If you have trouble locating a Food First title, write, call, or email us:

FOOD FIRST
398 60th Street
Oakland, CA 94618, USA
PHONE 510.654.4400
FAX 510.654.4551
EMAIL foodfirst@foodfirst.org
WEB www.foodfirst.org

If you are a bookseller or other reseller, contact our distributor, CDS, at 800.343.4499, to order.

Joining Food First

❏ I want to join Food First and receive a 20% discount on this and all subsequent orders. Enclosed is my tax-deductible contribution of:

❏ $35   ❏ $50   ❏ $100   ❏ $1,000   ❏ OTHER

NAME _____

ADDRESS _____

CITY/STATE/ZIP _____

DAYTIME PHONE (_____)_____

EMAIL _____

ORDERING FOOD FIRST MATERIALS

ITEM DESCRIPTION	QTY	UNIT COST	TOTAL

PAYMENT METHOD:

❏ CHECK

❏ MONEY ORDER

❏ MASTERCARD

❏ VISA

MEMBER DISCOUNT 20% $ _____

CA RESIDENTS SALES TAX 8.75% $ _____

SUBTOTAL $ _____

POSTAGE 15% • UPS 20% ($2 MIN.) $ _____

MEMBERSHIP(S) $ _____

ADDITIONAL CONTRIBUTION $ _____

TOTAL ENCLOSED $ _____

NAME ON CARD _____

CARD NUMBER _____ EXP. DATE _____

SIGNATURE _____

MAKE CHECK OR MONEY ORDER PAYABLE TO:
FOOD FIRST • 398 60TH STREET, OAKLAND, CA 94618

For gift memberships and mailings, please see coupon on reverse side.

Food First Gift Books

Please send a gift book to (order form on reverse side):

NAME _____

ADDRESS _____

CITY/STATE/ZIP _____

FROM _____

Food First Publications Catalogs

Please send a publications catalog to:

NAME _____

ADDRESS _____

CITY/STATE/ZIP _____

NAME _____

ADDRESS _____

CITY/STATE/ZIP _____

NAME _____

ADDRESS _____

CITY/STATE/ZIP _____

Food First Gift Memberships

❏ Enclosed is my tax-deductible contribution of:

❏ $35   ❏ $50   ❏ $100   ❏ $1,000   ❏ OTHER

Please send a Food First membership to:

NAME _____

ADDRESS _____

CITY/STATE/ZIP _____

FROM _____